SIGNS OF NEW LIFE

JOSEPH RATZINGER
BENEDICT XVI

Signs of New Life

Homilies on the
Church's Sacraments

With an Introduction by
BISHOP STEFAN OSTER, S.D.B.

Selected and edited by
MANUEL SCHLÖGL

TRANSLATED BY MICHAEL J. MILLER

IGNATIUS PRESS   SAN FRANCISCO

Original German edition:
Zeichen des neuen Lebens:
Predigten zu den Sakramenten der Kirche
© 2017 by Johannes Verlag Einsiedeln, Freiburg im Breisgau

Cover art:

The Baptism of Christ
Toros of Toron (13th–14th century A.D.)
The Matendaran Library
Yerevan, Armenia
© Scala/Art Resource, New York

Cover design by Roxanne Mei Lum

© 2020 by Libreria Editrice Vaticana
© 2020 by Ignatius Press, San Francisco
All rights reserved
ISBN 978-1-62164-297-8 (PB)
ISBN 978-1-64229-116-2 (eBook)
Library of Congress Control Number 2019952980
Printed in the United States of America ∞

Contents

ANOINTING OF THE SICK

MATRIMONY

HOLY ORDERS

Foreword by the Editor

The celebration of the Church's sacraments, even in our "secular age" (Charles Taylor), is still an occasion on which many people encounter God's saving work. Now as before there is a demand for Baptisms and weddings, First Communion and Confirmation; confession is experiencing a renaissance in many places; the Anointing of the Sick is often received with relatives and friends in attendance. Wherever sacraments are celebrated, they are also an opportunity to proclaim and deepen the faith.

Someone who preaches when the sacraments are administered must not only have experience in dealing with the word of God and with the historical-critical and spiritual exegesis of Scripture, but also have the ability to interpret the signs and symbolic actions, the rites and gestures in which God's invisible grace becomes visible and efficacious.

Joseph Ratzinger/Benedict XVI endeavored as a theologian to develop the hermeneutics of the sacraments in a new way and to make fruitful the participation of others in the celebration of them. Last but not least, many of his homilies refer to individual sacraments and connect them with a profound interpretation of Scripture and of the Christ event.

For this volume, two texts were selected from his homiletic work for each of the seven sacraments; the selections illuminate different aspects of the sacramental event and thus complement one another. The fourteen homilies are framed by two texts on the topic "Church", since all the sacraments are celebrated in the Church and there make visible their commission to be "sign and instrument [of] union with God" (*Lumen gentium* 1). The scriptural passages interpreted in each homily are listed at the beginning, so that the volume can also be used for scriptural meditation and spiritual reading.

My thanks, first of all, to the Pope Emeritus, Benedict XVI, who reviewed once again the previously unpublished texts and with his characteristic generosity agreed to their publication; to the private secretary of His Holiness, Archbishop Georg Gänswein, for his kind assistance; to my diocesan ordinary, Bishop Stefan Oster, S.D.B., for his substantial introduction; and last but not least to the publishing house Johannes Verlag for suggesting this book and for their usual helpful collaboration.

I dedicate this volume of homilies to the Bishop Emeritus of Passau, Wilhelm Schraml. Through priestly ordination, he called me to the special sacramental ministry, and as bishop he celebrated and proclaimed the Church's sacraments as what they are: signs of new life in Christ.

> Passau, on the Solemnity of the
> Assumption of the Blessed Virgin Mary, 2017
> *Rev. Dr. Manuel Schlögl*

Introduction

Salvation history in the fragments

"The whole in the fragment" is the title of a famous book by the Swiss theologian Hans Urs von Balthasar, who develops in it various "aspects of the theology of history", as the subtitle says.[1] In little things, in the fragmentary, in the concrete event within passing time, it is possible to get in contact with the whole, with the meaning of history, which is revealed to us in faith as salvation history. But this contact is possible only in such a way that we could never survey the meaning of the whole from our perspective, much less manipulate it to make it our own history. We can, however, get involved in it here and now by simply being there, present concretely in the flesh, listening to God's word, and obediently setting out on the way in front of us: accepting the gifts that are given to us and the tasks that are assigned to us. And so we become participants, partners, pilgrims on the way in God's great plan for his history—toward the salvation that he prepared for his people and each individual person. Insofar as we allow our individual story to be enfolded in God's ways with his people, the whole will shine forth, too, in each individual story of faith: the fact that God is

[1] Hans Urs von Balthasar, *Das Ganze im Fragment: Aspekte der Geschichtstheologie*, 2nd ed. (Einsiedeln: Johannes Verlag, 1990).

present through his faithful ones and leads them together in history as a whole toward perfection. And it will dawn on us that man first finds his real freedom and wins it permanently by being rooted in this way.

Are there nodal points in life?

But are there such things as decisive nodal points, in which man's contact with the eternal shines forth more clearly than in average everyday life, work, and leisure? From time immemorial, such very significant nodal points have included the beginning and the end of life, the transition from childhood to adult life, the mutual discovery and union of lovers, and also the transformation of life through a deeper insight into its real meaning. Man's profound awareness that he is more than a mere product of nature, more than an accidental being that arrives in the biological stream of life and disappears again, was expressed in the myths and religious rites of the nations, so that these nodal points were fraught with significance that towers over the individual person himself. Man already is always greater than his individual existence; he is most profoundly a communal being and always goes beyond himself into his community. But he also goes beyond himself into what was thought or believed to be heaven or the realm of the dead.

Christ gives the decisive explanation and direction

Now Christians believe that this original human belief in an origin and inkling of a destination that surpasses this life are decisively explained and directed in the coming of Jesus Christ. God himself arrives, becomes a man, and thus shows in an unsurpassable way who man is and who he can really be. Even more: Christ comes from the Father and goes back to the Father, but he wants us, his human brothers and sisters, to become once again children of the Father and to be reconciled with him. God is originally the Father of all mankind, but fallen humanity has gone astray and no longer knows about this original status as children. Man lives in the state of alienation, sin, egocentrism, fear of disappearing in death. Christ is in the most profound sense possible first of all the only Son of the Father. But he wants to be united with mankind as our brother in such a way that the Father can again see his only begotten Son in his creatures and rejoice in him. Christ enters into his creation permanently as a man—and even as the glorified Christ, he still remains a man.

Revaluation of the bodily condition

Hence, through the fact that he becomes man—and consequently is made flesh—all matter, too, everything material, experiences a profound affirmation. Whereas the mythical, philosophical, or religious experience of mankind that preceded Christ all too often was determined by the belief that matter and consequently the human bodily condition could be an obstacle for the spirit as it strove to lift itself up to the heights of the divine, this faith changes radically with Christ. Now, in him and henceforth in all who belong to him, he reveals that the human body itself is an expression of the spirit; the body is interpreted and experienced as a temple of God (see 1 Cor 6:19), because Christ himself sanctified the "temple of his body" (Jn 2:21).

"To the close of the age"

Therefore, the aforementioned historical nodal points of a human life—birth and death, loving union and transition to adulthood—can become specially sanctified moments through an interior union with the Lord and an external material sign. Christ walks with us through history—"to the close of the age" (Mt 28:20)—and at the prominent points of our life, his brothers and sisters can rely in faith on this presence with a special concentration: sacramentally. In Baptism and the Anointing of the Sick, in Confirmation and Matrimony, in the conversion of Penance.

The meal and the Eucharist

Christ radically pervades the material world: this is fully disclosed in two additional sacraments. In the Eucharist, the Lord uses a human meal, and thus also the everyday process of eating, in which man incorporates the material world into himself in a very fundamental sense and is nourished by it. The human meal, however, was always more than merely eating; a meal always established fellowship, also, participation in another's life, life as receiving the fruits of the earth, which are thus lifted up into man's cultural life form.

Jesus gives himself now as food. He uses bread and wine

so as to transform himself into them and thus to help man to be transformed again and again. The concrete history of the individual's walk with Christ finds in the Eucharistic meal again and again its most substantial encounter and form of spiritualization. So much so that it reverses the process of assimilation in eating: The person who eats bread transforms the bread into food that builds up the human body. The person who receives the Bread of Life, however, is transformed by Christ into someone who builds up his body, the Body of Christ, the Church.

Fully taken in possession

In ordination to the ministry of the deacon, priest, and bishop, finally, we believe that through the imposition of hands on the candidate for ordination Christ himself explicitly takes possession of him. Christ defines him explicitly and publicly as someone who can act in his name; someone who will make Christ present especially in preaching, in the Eucharist, and in forgiving sins. The individual man is called to renounce and to leave many things behind for Christ's sake. And he will be sent back a changed man, marked with the seal of the priest—and thus with the commission to give something that he himself does not have on his own: the Lord's presence in the Blessed Sacrament.

The Church herself is a sacrament

All sacraments, but particularly the Eucharist, are so central to our faith, our tradition, our Church, that the

Second Vatican Council said that the Church as a whole is a sacrament, namely, "a sign and instrument both of a very closely knit union with God and of the unity of the whole human race" (*Lumen gentium* 1).

An ecclesial and therefore sacramental existence

And Joseph Ratzinger/Pope Benedict XVI, for his part, as servant of the Church in such a variety of ministries over the course of his life and as preacher of God's word, stood and now stands so close to the heart of the Church that his homilies, too, always have a sacramental character, even when they do not speak explicitly about the sacraments. One senses that the word of proclamation in his case comes from recollection, from prayer, from the life that he leads existentially and corporeally in the presence of God. The word that he preaches always sheds new light on concrete human day-to-day living and makes it transparent to the working and presence of God in it. It is in this sense an "anointed word", for it illuminates not only by the power of outstanding theological thought, but above all by life in the Spirit, by life with the Lord in his Church. Anyone who becomes involved with this word of proclamation can tell how in such comprehensive and (in this sense) catholic thought and faith the concrete detail always opens onto the whole and also reveals this whole step by step: the whole in the fragment.

The discerning word

And it is a discerning word, through this word, spirits are separated and discerned again and again. What is lasting and eternal acquires its due weight; what is merely provisional and passing, but above all what gleams ambiguously or is irrelevant, is put in its place. Saint Thomas Aquinas emphasizes right at the beginning of his *Summa contra gentiles* that it is the task of the wise man to order things correctly.[2] That may sound a bit trivial, but the kind of order found in the homilies of Joseph Ratzinger shows that it is by no means insignificant. In his wisdom, he has penetrated deeply into the many individual areas of theological knowledge and disciplines and brought them into a truly ecclesial synthesis—and consequently he makes it impressively clear, again and again, that in the Catholic faith everything is interdependent—and that all of Christian life can be called sacramental.

Language as a litmus test

One more remark about the language of Joseph Ratzinger/ Benedict XVI. The wise man's task is not just to order but also to make comprehensible. And especially a preacher's way of speaking about theological knowledge and truths indicates whether and how he himself has taken this truth to heart or whether his speech is only a clever intellectual concept, which however can scarcely move its listeners. Basically the preacher, after all, in every homily speaks also to people with very different backgrounds in their heritage, education, faith, or theological insight.

[2] Thomas Aquinas, *Summa contra gentiles* I, 1 (Quod sit officium sapientis): ". . . ut sapientes dicantur qui res directe ordinant. . . ." Cited here from the one-volume Latin-German edition, ed., trans., and annotated by Karl Albert et al., 3rd ed. (Darmstadt: Wissenschaftliche Buchgesellschaft, 2009).

The homily is therefore always also an indication of two things: the preacher's love for what he is proclaiming and for those whom he is addressing. It is therefore something like a litmus test for all theology: Can a theologian reveal the height of the faith to the simple believer, too? And do so without trivializing the exalted truth? And can he also help the simple believer in the very concrete circumstances of life, explain the sacramental character of this very life for the believer? In my opinion, the homilies of Joseph Ratzinger/Benedict XVI are often a masterly textbook example of this; moreover, an example that finds expression not only in clear terms but at the same time in very beautiful language. And of course it is a textbook example that one cannot imitate simply by learning a technique. This ability is manifested, so to speak, as a result of the harmony of the heart in prayer, in life with other people, in the life of the Church, and in pondering Scripture and theology. And the Spirit of God makes his decisive contribution to it, too! With Joseph Ratzinger/Pope Benedict, that can be seen very clearly: how in his preaching, too, the whole is manifested in the fragmentary individual detail, precisely because it was obviously granted to him as a person, too, to bring his life, his action, his thought, and his language into an astonishing harmony.

My sincere thanks to Dr. Manuel Schlögl, a diocesan priest of Passau and a young scholar of the new *Schülerkreis* [circle of students] of Joseph Ratzinger/Pope Benedict XVI, that by selecting and editing these homilies on the sacraments he gives all of us new access to the intellectual and spiritual treasury of that great man, who likewise had his original home in our Diocese of Passau.

I wish the readers of these homilies much profit in head-knowledge and even more in heart-knowledge.

Passau, Pentecost 2017

Stefan Oster, S.D.B.
Bishop of Passau

What Holds It All Together—
Church as Foundation of Faith

1 Cor 3:1–9

"You are . . . God's building" (1 Cor 3:9). This statement by Saint Paul, which we just heard in the reading, is the basis for the whole ceremony of dedicating a church. This dedication intends, as it were, to elaborate this statement and to make its significance visible. We people, the faithful, are the real Church, the place in which God can find a dwelling. Among living people God can find an abode. The house that is built represents, so to speak, what we are. It can be Church only when we people fill it with our faith, with our worship, with hope and love, when the living Church makes it become Church. On the other hand, this house helps us to be Church by gathering us, by leading us to the Lord. The house represents *us*, and the consecration of the church intends to show how almost all the elements of this building point to our Christian existence, to its duties and its ways. I would like to single out from this wealth of signs only three elements: The church has walls, it has doors, and it has a cornerstone, a foundation, a construction that holds it all together—the exterior and the interior, what is above and what is below—and makes it one building.

The church has walls. On the one hand, the wall points inward; it is there to shelter, to gather, to lead us to each other. Its basic idea is to bring us together from the distractions in which we live outside, from the opposition in which we so often get lost, and to give us togetherness, both to lead us to responsibility for one another and also to give us the gift and the consolation of fellowship in faith and in the drama of human life. This is why the Church Fathers said that in the final analysis we ourselves are walls and can be so only if we are willing to let ourselves be cut like stones, to allow ourselves to be fitted together and precisely in this way, by letting ourselves be cut and fitted together, to move out of the merely private sphere. By becoming a wall, we can also receive the gift of being a building, of being carried and supported just as we carry and support others. The wall looks inward, it is something positive, it gathers, protects, unites. But it has another aspect, too: it looks outward, it draws a boundary, it keeps out what does not belong inside. At the height of the council—when this idea was becoming increasingly unfamiliar and in the optimism of the new openness, the opinion emerged that there were no boundaries at all, that there must be none—the Lutheran Evangelical Bishop Wilhelm Stählin gave a rousing lecture on the topic "Jerusalem Has Walls and Doors." He reminded us of the fact that even the Holy City of the end times, which is sketched in the Revelation of John, has walls, although its gates always stand open. That there are things that cannot go inside, must not go inside, lest the peace and freedom of this city be destroyed. John hints at these things against which the walls stand in the mysterious verse: "Outside are the dogs and sorcerers and fornicators and murderers and idolaters, and every one who loves and practices falsehood" (Rev 22:15). Stählin reflected on the question of what this is supposed to mean and quoted a verse by the Roman poet Juvenal: "Consider it the utmost corruption to prize life more than reverence." Lack of reverence does not belong inside, the cynicism to which nothing is sacred, that cannot bow, cannot remain silent, cannot show reverence, reduces what is great to what is common, no longer recognizes dignity, and consequently drags man down into the mud. Against this stand the walls, and they stand against the idolaters. What this means today becomes clear from a remark by Saint Paul. He once wrote: "covetousness . . . is idolatry" (Col 3:5). For idolatry, after all, means that we no longer acknowledge a supreme being over ourselves and think, instead, that the most important thing is to be able to get the most out of life; that possessing becomes the most important thing, that we kneel down before things and worship them, and thus upset the order of creation, turn it upside down, and destroy peace.

Falsehood must not enter, either; it destroys trust and makes communion impossible. Hatred and greed must not enter, for they injure humanity. *Against these* stand the walls of the Church, so as to build up the city of peace, freedom, and unity.

This brings us back again to the Fathers of the Church and to the rite of the dedication of a church, in which the wall is regarded as the presence of the twelve apostles. The saints are the walls that stand around us. They are the ones who are impervious to the spirit of wickedness, to lying, to licentiousness, to falsehood and hatred. They are the ones who at the same time are agents of invitation, who are permeable to everything that is good, great, and noble. The saints are a wall and at the same time a door, and we ourselves in all sobriety should be such saints, that is, people who are a wall for one another, people who keep away what is contrary to humanity and to the Lord, while they stand wide open for everything in us that means seeking, asking, and hoping.

Thus the sign of the wall coincides with the sign of the door. Before the bishop walks through the door to dedicate a church, he celebrates a door-liturgy, as it corresponds to the oldest tradition of mankind. It is taken from the prayer and faith of Israel, which in turn adopted the door-liturgy from pagan liturgies, while purifying and transforming it. Essentially, the bishop makes the Sign of the Cross on the threshold and thus makes visible the fact that the real door is the Cross. And only if we enter into the Cross, only if we go in with the Lord, and only if we are willing, in the Cross, to let what is contrary to God be taken from us—only then is the door open and do we truly enter in.

Another part of the door-liturgy is a chorus taken from Israel's door-liturgy in Psalm 24, which says, "Who shall ascend the hill of the LORD? And who shall stand in his holy place? He who has clean hands and a pure heart, who does not lift up his soul to what is false, and does not swear deceitfully" (Ps 24:3–4). Thus the door, too, is open and closed at the same time. It is meant to keep out anything that opposes what the Church is, and at the same time it is meant to be an invitation to become a door ourselves and to go through the door leading to the Father that Jesus Christ has become for us. Whenever we set foot in church, we perform a short door-liturgy following an old custom. We take holy water, go back to our Baptism, go back to the Cross, which is the true door to the Lord and consequently to each other, into the holy city Jerusalem, into the Church of God.

And finally the church has a foundation, a supporting force that holds the whole thing together. This final supporting force, the cornerstone and the capstone at the same time, is Christ.

Saint Thérèse of Lisieux once wrote: " 'I need a heart burning with tenderness, Who will be my support forever, Who loves everything in me, even my weakness . . . And who never leaves me day or night.' I could find no creature Who could always love me and never die. I must have a God who takes on my nature and becomes my brother and is able to suffer!" (Thérèse of Lisieux, "To the Sacred Heart of Jesus"). In these verses by the saint, the reader senses the aftereffects of what she suffered as a child when her mother, whom she loved above all else, was snatched away from her, and then one after another her two sisters who had become a mother to her. She experienced again and again the breakdown, the transience of love, without which we cannot live. The reader hears her cry for a love that no one can take from her, for a heart that is always there, that always understands me and shares in my sorrow, and the knowledge that no creature remains with us forever, that we need God, who is at the same time is man, who becomes clay, who suffers.

This is most profoundly Church: God's entrance, his arrival among us, his coming into the clay of this earth.

But at the same time he is the Christ, who is taken down from the Cross, who ascends, in whom the clay becomes spirit and glory and is drawn into God. Wherever we encounter the Crucified Lord, descent becomes ascent, our clay receives a place in God's glory. Wherever Christ is, there is transformation. Church is God's arrival among us and our arrival at him, through which transformation occurs, through which despair becomes hope and in the midst of being eternally deprived of all love, in the midst of the unreliability of all creatures, the reliability of his being-there holds us, too. Christ is in the Church not only as a picture; he is really there. Day after day, this descent of the Lord from the splendor of his glory, his stepping out and stepping in to us, and our ascent to him are accomplished on the altar. In the tabernacle, the altar is, so to speak, always alive, always remains Eucharist, always the entrance and ascent of Jesus Christ. Through him the church is always Church and never a lifeless house in which nothing is happening at the moment. He is there always. Over the centuries, it was always the great and beautiful thing about our churches that they stood open, that the door was really a door. It can stand open only if we ourselves stand open and our life constantly leads to him, when we, too, in our everyday routine have time for the mystery of his living closeness.

So let us ask him that this arrival of his may affect us, may carry us away, transform us, and make us truly become his living Church.

BAPTISM

The Light of Life

Rom 6:3–11

When the Church celebrates Easter, for her it is not a memory of something long past. If that were so, then we would have to admit that Rudolf Bultmann was right when he remarked: What difference could one man risen from the dead make among the harvest of millions of the dead throughout history? But the main word of the Easter liturgy is *hodie*—today. Today it happens. And when it says "today", in her view this is not meant theatrically, as though in the liturgy we identify playfully with what took place then and thus escape reality. Liturgy is not supposed to be a game but, rather, is an act of stepping into the genuine reality, stepping out of the half-reality in which we live, which continuously falls apart and passes away into nothing, and into the reality that is so real that it lasts. Liturgy is supposed to be, not less, but more reality. From time to time, people dream that it would be nice if we not only could travel through the vast extent of the universe but also had a vehicle with which we could wander through the ages and become contemporaneous

with them. Something like this can happen in the mystery
of the liturgy. It can happen because the Resurrection of
Jesus is not past; rather, by the Resurrection, he is in fact
elevated from what is passing into what is lasting, into
what is enduring. The Risen One is today, and if we can
touch him, then we can touch the today of the Resurrection, we can enter into the day of Resurrection that no
longer comes to an end, which has no evening, because
death no longer ends it.

According to the Church's faith, this can happen through
the sacraments. In the Paschal sacraments of Baptism,
Confirmation, and Eucharist, we can come into the Today of the Resurrection, touch the hand of the Risen
Lord, and thus become truly contemporary with Easter.
And in a special way this is true of Baptism, because it
is indeed the exit from a fallen life that is doomed to
death into perpetual living communion with Christ, as
we just heard in the reading from Saint Paul, who describes Baptism as communion with Christ's death and
Resurrection, as the Today of Easter day in the lives of
Christians. This is why since the earliest times the Easter
Vigil has been the Church's night for Baptism, in which
Easter happens here and now and is not just a memory
of a past time.

Now, of course, when we hear something like this, it is
difficult for us to accept. Our idea of the sacraments has
become much more moderate. What was just said leads
so far beyond our everyday notions that it takes consider-
able effort for us to realize its import. We have trimmed
the meaning of the sacraments to fit the comprehensible
context of our life. When parents have their children baptized today, it is often the case that they scarcely think

about this resurrection fellowship with Christ, but just want to emphasize the moment of birth with a bit more solemnity than the mere family celebration could give to it. The thought that they would rather not cut themselves off from a tradition that was sacred to their ancestors may play a role: there might still be something to it! Another factor might be the idea that they would like to entrust this young, defenseless life, which now steps over the threshold into a future full of unknown dangers, to a higher protector who perhaps exists. In any case, there is still the idea that through Baptism the child is accepted into the fellowship of the Church, into a living congregation that can offer him support and help in his life.

Modern theologians have even come up with the idea that Baptism is actually only admission to the Church, and because most people back then were not able to write, instead of a certificate, the Church gave them a solemn public act that necessarily made a great impression on everyone's memory. But by demoting Baptism, so to speak, to a somewhat naïve precursor of bureaucracy, the theologians now have really missed the heart of the matter and have understood less than is still surmised in the other reflections that I mentioned.

For in fact it is true that man at the moment of his physical birth is not born finished, because he is a physical and a spiritual being. Therefore, the process of his birth is necessarily a physical and a spiritual one. Therefore, he can be brought to his end and his goal only in open, understanding coexistence with other people. The biologist Adolf Portmann at the University of Basel has shown very incisively in biological studies how in a person the time of his conception and birth extends far into his conscious life, because another part of becoming himself is learning to walk upright, to listen, and to speak. These events, however, can occur only in coexistence with other people, since they are events and yet at the same time processes of spiritual acceptance and response.

In order for a man to be truly born, he must be there not only physically. He must be released so as to become himself, and, on the other hand, he must be accepted into a community of speaking, listening, living, and thinking. He needs release, he needs acceptance, and he needs in both the guideline of a meaning that supports his life. Man is a being who seeks meaning, and for him the meaning by which he can live, which animates him and gives him direction, is a condition of his physical existence; it is a part of him like the air that he breathes. He needs the guideline of a meaning, without which the gift of life would be meaningless and unjustifiable. But meaning is really given to him only if this meaning is stronger than death, if it is more life than physical life, for the meaning is the real life.

André Malraux, the friend of Charles de Gaulle, wrote down in his book about the human condition the sentence: "You know the phrase: It takes nine months to make a man and a single day to kill him." And he adds: "Listen: it does not take nine months, it takes fifty years to make a man. . . . And when this man is complete, . . . when he is really a man—he is good for nothing but to die."[1]

---

[1] André Malraux, *Man's Fate*, trans. Haakon M. Chevalier (New York: Random House, 1968; First Vintage International, 1990), 356.

And Augustine once said: "As when medical men examine an illness, and ascertain that it is fatal, they make this announcement; 'He will die, he will not get over this.' So from the moment of a man's birth, it may be said, '[Non evadet] He will not get over this.' "[2]

In these statements, it becomes clear that man, who is threatened by death, who advances toward nothingness, needs the meaning that withstands even the unknown powers of the future and is stronger than death. Only then is he really born, when there is a meaning that can defy this "non evadet"—"he will not escape it."

And this is precisely what happens in the Lord's Resurrection, which in Baptism becomes our meaning. The Resurrection of the Lord means that he is in person the truth of the statement: "Love is stronger than death." And Baptism means that he approaches us and takes us into the communion of life that no death has in its power. And so Baptism alone, the gift of meaning that gives an answer to death and is mightier than it, is the real, the new, the true birth, the true life.

The Church's baptismal liturgy, as we are about to experience it, suggests this in a variety of symbols. First in the symbol of water. Water is a symbol for the power of death. This shows that Baptism is not just about bureaucracy, about acceptance into an association that can be certified. And the baptismal water is more, too, than a washing; it is more than a cosmetic beautification of life.

[2] See Augustine, *Sermons on New Testament Lessons* 97, 3, 3, in *Nicene and Post-Nicene Fathers*, First Series, vol. 6, *Augustine: Sermon on the Mount, Harmony of the Gospels, Homilies on the Gospels*, ed. Philip Schaff (1888; Peabody, Mass.: Hendrickson, 1995), 412.

It is a death event. That is the order of magnitude about which the Church, in communion with the Risen Lord, is concerned. And only when this communion exists, in which what is at stake is not just conviviality or cosmetics but rather an answer to the question about death, is it worthwhile living; then this communion is a gift of meaning that extends into eternal life and hence makes the present life possible.

And along with this, then, the symbols of the white garment and the burning candle stand for the new life that is given. In one of her legends, Selma Lagerlöf depicts an Italian knight who is so ill-mannered that everyone finds him insufferable. One day he resolves to light a candle at the Holy Sepulcher in Jerusalem and to bring it home to Italy intact. Well, as he sets out on this pilgrimage and lives now only for the votive light, and is dedicated exclusively to this light and to making sure that it remains lit, what happens is not an outward journey but an inward journey. In this dedication to the light, he becomes free of himself and he himself becomes bright, because he must preserve what is given to him (Selma Lagerlöf, *Die Lichtflamme*).

This legend comes true in us in Baptism. Our candle, the light of meaning, of lasting life, is lit by the Risen Christ, and this is the great commission of our life: that we carry this light through it unquenched, during which time we, being dedicated to it, become ourselves.

May we, in this hour of the Church's Paschal Alleluia, allow ourselves to be moved anew by this joy of the Easter candle, which is our grace and our mission.

Our Yes to Christ

Mk 1:7–11

Dear Parents and Godparents,
Dear Brothers and Sisters,

What happens in Baptism? What do we hope for from Baptism? You have given a response on the threshold of this Chapel: We hope for eternal life for our children. This is the purpose of Baptism. But how can it be obtained? How can Baptism offer eternal life? What is eternal life?

In simpler words, we might say: we hope for a good life, the true life, for these children of ours; and also for happiness in a future that is still unknown. We are unable to guarantee this gift for the entire span of the unknown future, so we turn to the Lord to obtain this gift from him.

We can give two replies to the question, "How will this happen?" This is the first one: through Baptism each child is inserted into a gathering of friends who never abandon him in life or in death because these companions are God's family, which in itself bears the promise of eternity.

This group of friends, this family of God, into which the child is now admitted, will always accompany him, even on days of suffering and in life's dark nights; it will give him consolation, comfort, and light.

This companionship, this family, will give him words of eternal life, words of light in response to the great challenges of life, and will point out to him the right path to take. This group will also offer the child consolation and comfort, and God's love when death is at hand, in the dark valley of death. It will give him friendship, it will give him life. And these totally trustworthy companions will never disappear.

No one of us knows what will happen on our planet, on our European Continent, in the next fifty, sixty, or seventy years. But we can be sure of one thing: God's family will always be present, and those who belong to this family will never be alone. They will always be able to fall back on the steadfast friendship of the One who is life.

And, thus, we have arrived at the second answer. This family of God, this gathering of friends, is eternal, because it is communion with the One who conquered death and holds in his hand the keys of life. Belonging to this circle, to God's family, means being in communion with Christ, who is life and gives eternal love beyond death.

And if we can say that love and truth are sources of life, are life itself—and a life without love is not life— we can say that this companionship with the One who is truly life, with the One who is the Sacrament of life, will respond to your expectation, to your hope.

Yes, Baptism inserts us into communion with Christ and therefore gives life, life itself. We have thus interpreted the first dialogue we had with him here at the entrance to the Sistine Chapel.

Now, after the blessing of the water, a second dialogue

of great importance will follow. This is its content: Baptism, as we have seen, is a gift; the gift of life. But a gift must be accepted, it must be lived.

A gift of friendship implies a "yes" to the friend and a "no" to all that is incompatible with this friendship, to all that is incompatible with the life of God's family, with true life in Christ.

Consequently, in this second dialogue, three "noes" and three "yeses" are spoken. We say "no" and renounce temptation, sin, and the devil. We know these things well, but perhaps, precisely because we have heard them too often, the words may not mean much to us.

If this is the case, we must think a little more deeply about the content of these "noes". What are we saying "no" to? This is the only way to understand what we want to say "yes" to.

In the ancient Church these "*noes*" were summed up in a phrase that was easy to understand for the people of that time: they renounced, they said, the "*pompa diabuli*", that is, the promise of life in abundance, of that apparent life that seemed to come from the pagan world, from its permissiveness, from its way of living as one pleased.

It was therefore "no" to a culture of what seemed to be an abundance of life, to what in fact was an "*anticulture*" of death. It was "no" to those spectacles in which death, cruelty, and violence had become an entertainment.

Let us remember what was organized at the Colosseum or here, in Nero's gardens, where people were set on fire like living torches. Cruelty and violence had become a form of amusement, a true perversion of joy, of the true meaning of life.

This *"pompa diabuli"*, this "anticulture" of death, was a corruption of joy, it was love of deceit and fraud and the abuse of the body as a commodity and a trade.

And if we think about it now, we can say that also in our time we need to say "no" to the widely prevalent culture of death.

It is an "anticulture" manifested, for example, in drugs, in the flight from reality to what is illusory, to a false happiness expressed in deceit, fraud, injustice, and contempt for others, for solidarity, and for responsibility for the poor and the suffering; it is expressed in a sexuality that becomes sheer irresponsible enjoyment, that makes the human person into a "thing", so to speak, no longer considered a person who deserves personal love which requires fidelity, but who becomes a commodity, a mere object.

Let us say "no" to this promise of apparent happiness, to this *"pompa"* of what may seem to be life but is in fact merely an instrument of death, and to this "anticulture", in order to cultivate instead the culture of life. For this reason, the Christian "yes", from ancient times to our day, is a great "yes" to life. It is our "yes" to Christ, our "yes" to the Conqueror of death and the "yes" to life in time and in eternity.

Just as in this baptismal dialogue the "no" is expressed in three renunciations, so too the "yes" is expressed in three expressions of loyalty: "yes" to the living God, that is, a God Creator and a creating reason who gives meaning to the cosmos and to our lives; "yes" to Christ, that is, to a God who did not stay hidden but has a name, words, a body, and blood; to a concrete God who gives us life and shows us the path of life; "yes" to the communion of the Church, in which Christ is the living God who enters our time, enters our profession, enters daily life.

We might also say that the Face of God, the content of this culture of life, the content of our great "yes", is expressed in the Ten Commandments, which are not a pack of prohibitions, of "noes", but actually present a great vision of life.

They are a "yes" to a God who gives meaning to life (the first three Commandments); a "yes" to the family (Fourth Commandment); a "yes" to life (Fifth Commandment); a "yes" to responsible love (Sixth Commandment); a "yes" to solidarity, to social responsibility, to justice (Seventh Commandment); a "yes" to the truth (Eighth Commandment); a "yes" to respect for others and for their belongings (Ninth and Tenth Commandments).

This is the philosophy of life, the culture of life that becomes concrete and practical and beautiful in communion with Christ, the living God, who walks with us in the companionship of his friends, in the great family of the Church. Baptism is a gift of life.

It is a "yes" to the challenge of really living life, of saying "no" to the attack of death that presents itself under the guise of life; and it is a "yes" to the great gift of true life that became present on the Face of Christ, who gives himself to us in Baptism and subsequently in the Eucharist.

I said this as a brief comment on the words in the baptismal dialogue that interpret what happens in this sacrament. In addition to the words, we have gestures and symbols, but I will just point them out very briefly.

We have already made the first gesture: it is the Sign of

the Cross, which is given to us as a shield that must protect this child in his life; and as an "indicator" that points out the way of life, for the Cross sums up Jesus' life.

Then, there are the elements: water, the anointing with oil, the white garment, and the flame of the candle.

Water is the symbol of life: Baptism is new life in Christ. The oil is the symbol of strength, health, and beauty, for it truly is beautiful to live in communion with Christ. Then, there is the white garment, as an expression of the culture of beauty, of the culture of life. And lastly, the flame of the candle is an expression of the truth that shines out in the darkness of history and points out to us who we are, where we come from, and where we must go.

Dear godparents, dear parents, dear brothers and sisters, let us thank the Lord today, for God does not hide behind clouds of impenetrable mystery but, as today's Gospel said, has opened the heavens, he has shown himself, he talks to us and is with us; he lives with us and guides us in our lives.

Let us thank the Lord for this gift and pray for our children, so that they may truly have life: authentic, eternal life. Amen.

CONFIRMATION

"Choose Life!"

Deut 30:15–20; Jn 14:1–6

The Church explains for us palpably what the Sacrament of Confirmation means in the signs with which it is administered. If we look a little more closely at the sequence of events in the Confirmation ceremony, we can easily determine that it is performed in three stages. It starts with the Confirmation promise; next comes the prayer that the bishop recites in the name of the Church with hands outstretched; and finally there is the actual administration of Confirmation, which includes anointing, imposition of hands, and the sign of peace. Let us look more closely at each of these three parts.

The ceremony begins with a question and answer session: "Do you renounce Satan, . . . do you believe in God, the Father Almighty, . . . in Jesus Christ, his only Son, . . . in the Holy Spirit, . . . [and] the holy catholic Church?" These questions link Confirmation and Baptism together. They were already asked at Baptism and for most of you were then answered vicariously by your parents and godparents, who so to speak lent you their

faith, just as they placed a bit of their life at your disposal
in the first place, so that body and soul and mind could
awaken and develop. But what was borrowed must now
be made your own: As people, of course, our lives de-
pend on each other, on what we do not just lend but give
to each other. One supports the other. Nevertheless, we
must also decide for ourselves; what is given to us belongs
to us only if we ourselves have accepted it. So Confirmation continues what began in Baptism. It is the comple-
tion of Baptism. This is even the actual meaning of the
word "Confirmation": it means the same as strengthen-
ing. "Confirmation" is a word from legal language and is
applied to the process by which a treaty definitively goes
into effect.

In fact, this promise with which the Confirmation ceremony begins is designed like the conclusion of a treaty.
It is reminiscent of the covenant that God made with
Israel on Mount Sinai. There God had confronted Israel
with a choice: "I have set before you life and death . . . ;
therefore choose life, that you and your descendants may
live" (Deut 30:19). Confirmation is your Sinai. The Lord
stands in front of you and says to you: Choose life! Everyone would like to live, to get as much as possible out of
life, to make the most of what life has to offer, as far as
possible. Choose life! We have really chosen life, then,
only if we are in a covenant with the one who is himself Life. The renunciation of Satan means the renunciation of the power of falsehood, which deceives us with
promises of life while leading us into the desert. For example, someone who gets trapped by drug abuse is looking for an undreamed-of expansion of life into fantastic,

limitless realms and thinks at first that he has found it,
too. But in reality, he is deceived; finally, he can no longer
bear real life, and then the other one, the lie into which
he was lured, falls apart, too. Choose life! The questions
and answers of the Confirmation promise are a sort of
introduction to life; they are the road signs for the ascent
to life, which is not always easy. But what is easy is not
what is true, and only what is true is life. We said earlier that this promise is a sort of a treaty, a covenant. We
could also say that it resembles a wedding. We place our
hand into the hands of Jesus Christ. We decide to walk
our way with him, because we know: He is the life (Jn
14:6).

Part of being a Christian is making decisions, but it
is not merely a system of commandments that demand
moral accomplishments of us. In being Christian, we are
also the ones being gifted. It means being accepted into a
community that supports us—the Church. This becomes
visible in the second act of the Confirmation ceremony,
the prayer that the bishop recites in the name of the whole
Church by virtue of his consecration. While doing so, the
bishop extends his hands, as Moses did while Israel was
fighting (Ex 17:11–12). These outstretched hands are like
a roof that covers and protects us from sun and rain; they
are also like an antenna that picks up the airwaves and thus
brings us together with what is in itself far removed from
us. In this way, the imposition of hands depicts what the
prayer means: As Christians we are always taken into the
prayer of the whole Church. No one stands alone. No
one is altogether forgotten and abandoned. Each one belongs to the community, which in prayer always takes

responsibility for all. Thus, this prayer really is like a roof; we stand under the protection of these outstretched hands. And it is like an antenna that brings what is distant close to us—what is distant, the power of the Holy Spirit, becomes ours, if we stand in the electric circuit of this prayer. The beautiful words that the father in the parable of the prodigal son says to the brother who remained home applies to someone who lives in the Church: "All that is mine is yours" (Lk 15:31). Just as at the beginning of our life our parents loaned us their lives and their faith, so too the Church holds us tight in her faith and her prayer; it belongs to us through the fact that we belong to her. Thus, even the great and seemingly so distant words acquire a meaning: the prayer for the Spirit of wisdom, fortitude, piety, fear of the Lord. No one can build his life alone; not even wisdom, knowledge, and the strength of the mightiest are enough to do that. All we need do is look at the newspapers to see again and again how the mighty and the much admired are often the ones who ultimately no longer know what to do with their lives and are ruined. If, conversely, we ask about the secret of people who perhaps were very simple, but found peace and fulfillment, then it is clear that the core of their secret is this: they were not alone. They did not have to invent life themselves. They did not need to think up what it means and how it goes. "Choose life!" They accepted "counsel" where counsel is to be found, and so they possessed what they themselves did not have: wisdom, fortitude, insight: "All that is mine is yours." They stood under a roof that covers but does not cut off; rather, it receives the airwaves of the Eternal One, the waves of life, and connects us with it. The bishop's hands show us where this roof is that we all need. They are an indicator and a promise: Under the roof of Confirmation, under the roof of the praying Church, we live safely and openly at the same time: in the electric circuit of the Holy Spirit.

It begins with the fact that each individual is called by his name. In God's sight, we are not a mass of humanity. Therefore, sacraments are never administered collectively, but always personally. For God, every individual has his own face, his own name. God speaks to us personally. We are not interchangeable samples of a commodity; we are friends—known, chosen, loved. God has his own plan for each one. He wants each one. No one is superfluous, no one is a mere accident. You should take that to heart during this calling of the names. God wants *me*. What does he want of me?

The imposition of hands is the application of the gesture of the outstretched hands to our personal space. The imposition of hands is initially a gesture of taking possession. If I place my hand on something, I mean by that to say: This is mine. The Lord places his hand on us. We are his. My life does not simply belong to me. I cannot say: This is *my* life; I can do with it what I want; if I mess it up, then that is my private concern. No, God has intended for me a task on behalf of the whole. If I destroy this life or fail at it, then something is lacking in the whole. From a negative life proceed negative influences for other people; from a positive life proceed blessings for the whole. No one lives for himself alone. My life is not mine. I am being asked: What did you do with this life that I gave you? His hand rests on me . . .

The imposition of hands, however, is also a gesture of tenderness or friendship. If I can say nothing more to a sick person because he is too tired, maybe even unconscious, but place my hand on him, he feels a closeness that helps him. He knows: I am not alone. The imposition of hands suggests at the same time God's tenderness toward us. Through this imposition of hands, I know: A love is supporting me on which I can rely unconditionally. A love is accompanying me that never disappoints me and does not let me fall even in my failure. An understanding is there that is certain for me, even when no one else wants to understand me. Someone has laid his hand on me—the Lord.

Imposing hands, moreover, is a protective gesture. The Lord takes responsibility for me. He does not spare me the wind and the weather, but he protects me from the real evil—which in all our definitions of protection we usually forget: the loss of faith, the loss of God—provided that I entrust myself to him and do not let go of his hand and run away.

Then the forehead is marked with the Sign of the Cross. It is the sign of Jesus Christ, in which he will someday come again. It is also a sign of ownership—being made over to Christ, as we promised earlier. It is a signpost. Along the streets stand road signs, so that a driver can find his destination when he travels. Our [Bavarian] ancestors were fond of setting up the image of the Crucified Lord along the streets, as a signpost, too. They meant to say: We are traveling not only from this village to that one, from this city to another. In all our journeys, our life is being spent and perfected. On all these paths our

life is being lived, and we must find not only particular
places, but life itself. That was the message of this odd
signpost: Beware, lest you finish your life at a dead end.
Follow this man, and then you will find the way, for he
is the Way (Jn 14:6). The Cross, however (and all this
goes together), is an invitation to prayer. With the Sign
of the Cross we start our prayers; the Eucharist begins
with it; with it absolution is given to us in the Sacrament of Penance. The cross of Confirmation invites us
to prayer, to both personal prayer and to the great communal prayer of the Eucharist. It tells us: You can return
to Confirmation again and again by returning to this sign.
Confirmation is not a momentary event; it is a beginning
that is meant to mature throughout a life. You enter into
Baptism and into Confirmation whenever you enter into
this sign. There, the prayer and the promise of this day
are fulfilled step by step: the coming of the Spirit of wisdom, understanding, counsel, and fortitude. You cannot
put this Spirit into your pocket like a coin and bring it
out as needed. You can receive him only by living with
him—at the point of contact that he himself has given
us: the cross.

   This cross is marked on our forehead with the sacred
chrism that the bishop consecrates on Holy Thursday for
a whole year and for a whole diocese. Several things come
to light in this custom. In the ancient world, oil was a
cosmetic; it was a basic food; it was the most important medicine; it protected the body against the burning
heat and thus at the same time fortified it. An element
of strength and preservation. In this way it became the
expression of the strength and beauty of life in general

and a symbol of the Holy Spirit. Prophets, kings, and priests were anointed with oil, so that oil also became a sign of these offices. In the language of Israel, the king was simply called "the Anointed"; the Greek word for this is "Christ". Thus the anointing once again means that Christ himself takes us into his hand; it means that he offers us life—the Holy Spirit. "Choose life"—that is not only a command; it is at the same time a gift. "Here it is", the Lord tells us in the Sign of the Cross that is administered with the oil.

Another important thing, though, is what we just heard: this oil is consecrated for the whole year and for all places on Holy Thursday. It comes from the decision to love that Christ expressed definitively at the Last Supper. This decision encompasses places and times. Someone who wants to belong to him cannot confine himself to a group, a congregation, a nation, a party. Only when we open ourselves up to the common faith of all places and times are we with him. Only when we believe together with the whole Church, take our standard from her, and do not hold up our own ideas as absolute are we included in the great electrical circuit of his life. Confirmation is always the transcending of boundaries, too. It demands that we give up the pettiness of our ideas and wishes, our "knowing better", and become truly "catholic": living, thinking, and acting with the whole Church. This has to have its effects, for example, in our co-responsibility for the poor of the whole world; it must have its effects in our prayer, in that we celebrate the liturgy of the whole Church and do not follow our own inspirations; it has to have its effects in the form of our faith, which takes it standard from the word of the whole Church and her tradition. We are not the ones who make the faith; the Lord gives it to us as a gift. He gives himself to us. The Sign of the Cross made with the sacred chrism is for us a guarantee that he takes us in hand and that his Spirit touches and leads us when we are with the Church.

Let us look back on everything that we have reflected on. It seems to me that the three-step structure of Confirmation is also a parable for the path of our Christian life. In the sequence: promise, prayer, sealing, first we ourselves act, then the Church, then Christ and the Holy Spirit. We can therefore describe the three parts also as word, response, and action; we—Church—Christ alternate as acting persons. The form of the sacrament reflects the rhythm of life. At the beginning, there is above all the challenge to perform our own action: to be a Christian appears as a decision, as a demand on our courage and our ability to renounce and to decide. It seems laborious, and other people's lives appear more comfortable. But the more we enter into the Yes of the baptismal and Confirmation promise, the more we experience the support of the Church as a whole. When what is my own, what I myself have made, and what I myself can do begin to fall apart, then the fruit of the response begins to appear. When for a person without God life becomes an empty husk that is best thrown away, a truth becomes increasingly evident: I am not alone. And even if it slowly grows dark, the path still leads to the love that embraces and holds us where no man can hold us any longer. Faith is the firm ground for the house of our life; it stands fast even in a future that no one can know in advance.

Thus Confirmation is a promise that reaches into eternity. But before that, it is an appeal to our courage and our bravery; an appeal to dare with Christ to build our life on him in the willingness of faith, even if other people find that ridiculous or old-fashioned. The way leads into the light.

Let us dare to follow it. Let us say Yes. This hour of the holy sacrament encourages us to do it: "Choose life!"

Sealed with the Spirit

Acts 2:1–11; 1 Cor 12:3b–7, 12–13; Lk 4:14–22a

Dear Friends,

"You will receive power when the Holy Spirit comes upon you" (Acts 1:8). We have seen this promise fulfilled! On the day of Pentecost, as we heard in the first reading, the Risen Lord, seated at the right hand of the Father, sent the Spirit upon the disciples gathered in the Upper Room. In the power of that Spirit, Peter and the Apostles went forth to preach the Gospel to the ends of the earth. In every age, and in every language, the Church throughout the world continues to proclaim the marvels of God and to call all nations and peoples to faith, hope, and new life in Christ.

In these days I, too, have come, as the Successor of Saint Peter, to this magnificent land of Australia. I have come to confirm you, my young brothers and sisters, in your faith and to encourage you to open your hearts to the power of Christ's Spirit and the richness of his gifts. I pray that this great assembly, which unites young people "from every nation under heaven" (cf. Acts 2:5), will be a new Upper Room. May the fire of God's love descend to fill your hearts, unite you ever more fully to the Lord and his Church, and send you forth, a new generation of apostles, to bring the world to Christ!

"You will receive power when the Holy Spirit comes upon you." These words of the Risen Lord have a special meaning for those young people who will be confirmed, sealed with the gift of the Holy Spirit, at today's Mass. But they are also addressed to each of us—to all those who have received the Spirit's gift of reconciliation and new life at Baptism, who have welcomed him into their hearts as their helper and guide at Confirmation, and who daily grow in his gifts of grace through the Holy Eucharist. At each Mass, in fact, the Holy Spirit descends anew, invoked by the solemn prayer of the Church, not only to transform our gifts of bread and wine into the Lord's body and blood, but also to transform our lives, to make us, in his power, "one body, one spirit in Christ".

But what is this "power" of the Holy Spirit? It is the power of God's life! It is the power of the same Spirit who hovered over the waters at the dawn of creation and who, in the fullness of time, raised Jesus from the dead. It is the power which points us, and our world, toward the coming of the Kingdom of God. In today's Gospel, Jesus proclaims that a new age has begun, in which the Holy Spirit will be poured out upon all humanity (cf. Lk 4:21). He himself, conceived by the Holy Spirit and born of the Virgin Mary, came among us to bring us that Spirit. As the source of our new life in Christ, the Holy Spirit is also, in a very real way, the soul of the Church, the love which binds us to the Lord and one another, and the light which opens our eyes to see all around us the wonders of God's grace.

Here in Australia, this "great south land of the Holy Spirit", all of us have had an unforgettable experience of the Spirit's presence and power in the beauty of nature. Our eyes have been opened to see the world around us as it truly is: "charged", as the poet says, "with the grandeur of God", filled with the glory of his creative love. Here too, in this great assembly of young Christians from all over the world, we have had a vivid experience of the Spirit's presence and power in the life of the Church. We have seen the Church for what she truly is: the Body of Christ, a living community of love, embracing people of every race, nation, and tongue, of every time and place, in the unity born of our faith in the Risen Lord.

The power of the Spirit never ceases to fill the Church with life! Through the grace of the Church's sacraments, that power also flows deep within us, like an underground river which nourishes our spirit and draws us ever nearer to the source of our true life, which is Christ. Saint Ignatius of Antioch, who died a martyr in Rome at the beginning of the second century, has left us a splendid description of the Spirit's power dwelling within us. He spoke of the Spirit as a fountain of living water springing up within his heart and whispering: "Come, come to the Father" [cf. *Epistle to the Romans*, 7, 2].

Yet this power, the grace of the Spirit, is not something that we can merit or achieve, but only receive as pure gift. God's love can only unleash its power when it is allowed to change us from within. We have to let it break through the hard crust of our indifference, our spiritual weariness, our blind conformity to the spirit of this age. Only then can we let it ignite our imagination and shape our deepest desires. That is why prayer is so important: daily prayer, private prayer in the quiet of our hearts and before the

Blessed Sacrament, and liturgical prayer in the heart of the Church. Prayer is pure receptivity to God's grace, love in action, communion with the Spirit who dwells within us, leading us, through Jesus, in the Church, to our heavenly Father. In the power of his Spirit, Jesus is always present in our hearts, quietly waiting for us to be still with him, to hear his voice, to abide in his love, and to receive "power from on high", enabling us to be salt and light for our world.

At his Ascension, the Risen Lord told his disciples: "You will be my witnesses . . . to the ends of the earth" (Acts 1:8). Here, in Australia, let us thank the Lord for the gift of faith, which has come down to us like a treasure passed on from generation to generation in the communion of the Church. Here, in Oceania, let us give thanks in a special way for all those heroic missionaries, dedicated priests and religious, Christian parents and grandparents, teachers and catechists who built up the Church in these lands—witnesses like Blessed Mary MacKillop, Saint Peter Chanel, Blessed Peter To Rot, and so many others! The power of the Spirit, revealed in their lives, is still at work in the good they left behind, in the society which they shaped and which is being handed on to you.

Dear young people, let me now ask you a question. What will *you* leave to the next generation? Are you building your lives on firm foundations, building something that will endure? Are you living your lives in a way that opens up space for the Spirit in the midst of a world that wants to forget God, or even rejects him in the name of a falsely-conceived freedom? How are you using the gifts you have been given, the "power" which the Holy

Spirit is even now prepared to release within you? What legacy will you leave to young people yet to come? What difference will you make?

The power of the Holy Spirit does not only enlighten and console us. It also points us to the future, to the coming of God's Kingdom. What a magnificent vision of a humanity redeemed and renewed we see in the new age promised by today's Gospel! Saint Luke tells us that Jesus Christ is the fulfillment of all God's promises, the Messiah who fully possesses the Holy Spirit in order to bestow that gift upon all mankind. The outpouring of Christ's Spirit upon humanity is a pledge of hope and deliverance from everything that impoverishes us. It gives the blind new sight; it sets the downtrodden free; and it creates unity in and through diversity (cf. Lk 4:18–19; Is 61:1–2). This power can create a new world: it can "renew the face of the earth" (cf. Ps 104:30)!

Empowered by the Spirit and drawing upon faith's rich vision, a new generation of Christians is being called to help build a world in which God's gift of life is welcomed, respected, and cherished—not rejected, feared as a threat, and destroyed. A new age in which love is not greedy or self-seeking, but pure, faithful, and genuinely free, open to others, respectful of their dignity, seeking their good, radiating joy and beauty. A new age in which hope liberates us from the shallowness, apathy, and self-absorption which deaden our souls and poison our relationships. Dear young friends, the Lord is asking you to be prophets of this new age, messengers of his love, drawing people to the Father and building a future of hope for all humanity.

The world needs this renewal! In so many of our so-
cieties, side by side with material prosperity, a spiritual
desert is spreading: an interior emptiness, an unnamed
fear, a quiet sense of despair. How many of our contem-
poraries have built broken and empty cisterns (cf. Jer 2:13)
in a desperate search for meaning—the ultimate meaning
that only love can give? This is the great and liberating
gift which the Gospel brings: it reveals our dignity as men
and women created in the image and likeness of God. It
reveals humanity's sublime calling, which is to find fulfillment in love. It discloses the truth about man and the
truth about life.

The Church also needs this renewal! She needs your
faith, your idealism, and your generosity, so that she can
always be young in the Spirit (cf. *Lumen gentium*, 4)! In
today's second reading, the Apostle Paul reminds us that
each and every Christian has received a gift meant for
building up the Body of Christ. The Church especially
needs the gifts of young people, all young people. She
needs to grow in the power of the Spirit who even now
gives joy to your youth and inspires you to serve the Lord
with gladness. Open your hearts to that power! I address
this plea in a special way to those of you whom the Lord
is calling to the priesthood and the consecrated life. Do
not be afraid to say "yes" to Jesus, to find your joy in
doing his will, giving yourself completely to the pursuit
of holiness, and using all your talents in the service of
others!

In a few moments, we will celebrate the Sacrament of
Confirmation. The Holy Spirit will descend upon the
confirmands; they will be "sealed" with the gift of the

Spirit and sent forth to be Christ's witnesses. What does it mean to receive the "seal" of the Holy Spirit? It means being indelibly marked, inalterably changed, a new creation. For those who have received this gift, nothing can ever be the same! Being "baptized" in the one Spirit (cf. 1 Cor 12:13) means being set on fire with the love of God. Being "given to drink" of the Spirit means being refreshed by the beauty of the Lord's plan for us and for the world, and becoming in turn a source of spiritual refreshment for others. Being "sealed with the Spirit" means not being afraid to stand up for Christ, letting the truth of the Gospel permeate the way we see, think, and act, as we work for the triumph of the civilization of love.

As we pray for the confirmands, let us ask that the power of the Holy Spirit will revive the grace of our own Confirmation. May he pour out his gifts in abundance on all present, on this city of Sydney, on this land of Australia, and on all its people! May each of us be renewed in the spirit of wisdom and understanding, the spirit of right judgment and courage, the spirit of knowledge and reverence, the spirit of wonder and awe in God's presence!

Through the loving intercession of Mary, Mother of the Church, may this Twenty-third World Youth Day be experienced as a new Upper Room, from which all of us, burning with the fire and love of the Holy Spirit, go forth to proclaim the Risen Christ and to draw every heart to him! Amen.

CONFESSION

Be Reconciled with God

2 Cor 5:17—6:2; Lk 4:16–21

"Today this Scripture has been fulfilled in your hearing" (Lk 4:21). This verse of the Gospel is true for us, too, in this hour. In the Holy Year 1983, we reflect that 1,950 years ago our Lord Jesus Christ was crucified for us and rose again. But this does not mean that we are thinking about a past event. The Holy Year is not one of the usual jubilees in which people look back at something that once was. During the Holy Year it is true: "Today this Scripture has been fulfilled." Redemption is not the past; it is God's Now for us, as we just heard also in the reading: "Now is the acceptable time; behold, now is the day of salvation" (2 Cor 6:2). This holy time says to us: We are redeemed. What Christ did is present and creates a future. Redemption is reality; it is the foundation of the confidence with which we enter into what is to come. Being redeemed means: We are accepted, we are loved. The powers of good are—contrary to all appearances—stronger than the powers of evil that are still so great. Therefore, it is good to be a human being. Therefore, we can be happy to be alive. Therefore, we will be able to thank God today and again tomorrow that the world exists, that man exists, that we have the privilege of living. Redemption, of course, is not something that covers us over externally, so to speak. Indeed, redemption itself wants us. That is why it opens up a path and takes us along with it on its way. The Holy Year intends not only to make all this visible, but also to make it a living reality in us.

The Holy Year interprets for us God's Today, which was our starting point, and his invitation to the way of the redeemed in three signs: in the sign of pilgrimage, in the sign of the Holy Door, and in the sign of the indulgence. I would like to try to say something briefly about these three signs, which are intended to make evident the one truth of the statement "We are redeemed."

First, there is the pilgrimage. Pilgrimage is one of the primordial gestures of mankind, as far as we can look back in general at its history. Man sets out again and again on the road. He seeks something greater. Even in his home he notices that he is not yet entirely at home, but still needs a journey in order really to come to himself and to come to God, for only in God's house is he truly at home with himself. Because such a profound truth is concealed in the primordial human gesture of seeking and being on the road, Israel received anew and in a new interpretation the command in God's revealed law to go on pilgrimage. At the threshold of the Holy Land, after the forty years of wandering in the desert, Israel was told: Even at home you should remain a nation of wanderers. Three times a year you should go to Jerusalem, as though constantly on the road from everyday routine into the other realm, into communion with God and with one another, and then return again from this greater realm to your everyday routine. You should remain wanderers, people on the road, who know that we are still looking for the definitive city. This custom of making pilgrimages in Israel had the purpose also of bringing this scattered people again and again to unity, to one another, and to make it experience the brotherhood of the twelve tribes of Israel. In this way, it was supposed to become one again and again based on the unity of the one God, who alone can ultimately establish unity and reconciliation among men.

Thus we can observe a multiple significance of the pilgrimage in Israel. It is about the unity of the people, about the visible representation of the unity of the one God. It is about staying on the road, not forgetting the transient character of all our things. Even in Christianity, all this is not outmoded. That is why pilgrimage is also one of the forms in which the Christian faith has been expressed from the earliest days. Indeed, it could not extinguish man's primordial yearning to find a way now and then out of the everyday routine, to gain some distance from it and to become free of it. This drive is still at work even in the later "secular brother" of pilgrimage, tourism. Because it continues to exist, these streams of wanderers roll ceaselessly over the continent. Man senses that he is not entirely at home. But pilgrimage must be more than tourism. It must accomplish better, more thoroughly, more purely what is intended in tourism. Part of this is, on the one hand, a greater simplicity and, on the other hand, a greater purposefulness. Part of pilgrimage is the simplicity that accepts being a pilgrim. For if we wish to consume just as much and have the same life-style everywhere, then we can travel around the world as far as we like, but we always remain at home. We can really experience "something different" only if we ourselves are different and live differently; if in the simplicity of faith we interiorly become pilgrims. Part of this is the intrinsic purposefulness of faith. On a pilgrimage, it is not all about sightseeing or some experiences or other that then nevertheless do not lead out of ourselves into something truly new. The goal of the pilgrimage is ultimately not sightseeing but setting out for the living God. We try to do this by visiting the sites of salvation history. The interior and exterior paths of pilgrimage do not run in a random direction. We travel, so to speak, into the geography of God's history, to places where he himself set up his path markers. We head for what has been marked out for us and not for what we ourselves have sought. By entering into his history and turning to the signs that the Church sets up for us in the full authority of her faith, we also go toward one another. By becoming pilgrims, we can receive better the thing that tourism is seeking: something different, distance, freedom, and a deeper encounter.

The second sign I would like to speak about is the Holy Door. This, too, is a sign that is deeply ingrained in mankind. We are all looking, so to speak, for the exit that leads to the open air, for the door through which we can finally come out into freedom. And at the same time, we are looking for the door that leads to security.

We seek to reach the place where freedom and security are side by side. Most profoundly, in this way we seek the lost paradise, which is inscribed in every human heart like a primordial memory. The door of the Holy Year of course does not symbolize the gates of paradise directly; rather, it is a reminder of the door through which we walked at the dawn of our life: the door of holy Baptism. When we came through the Holy Door into the church this morning, this should have been a challenge really to walk through the door of being-baptized, the door leading not only into the church that is built of stones but into the living Church. We walk through it in the Church's common faith, common life, common tasks, and common sufferings. In our life, the door of Baptism means above all: door of Penance. In order truly to be baptized Christians, we must, so to speak, stoop down again and again so as go through this door of Penance. How reassuring it is when we know that a person is working to improve himself; he knows about his faults and is trying to correct them henceforth. He looks for what is wrong not only in me but in himself, and tomorrow I will have a new beginning with him. How terrible it is, conversely, when someone no longer knows that he has faults. The door of Penance means for us that we let our eyes be opened, that self-righteousness is shattered, that we learn to stoop down, and that we thus become new, redeemed persons. The gate to Paradise is said to be guarded by the cherubim with the flaming sword (Gen 3:24). Penance means that in the grace of forgiveness we can walk through the flames without being burned *up*. We must in any case be *burned*, because there is much in us that must be refined

by fire. When we look at the sign of the door, finally, we
come upon the words of Jesus Christ: "I am the door"
(Jn 10:9). If we walk with him, if we get to know him, if
we go through the door into the open air, then we need
not fear even the last dark door at which our life will
arrive.

The third sign, the indulgence, actually sums up all this,
for by its nature it is an invitation to the pilgrimage, an
invitation to the sacrament, and an invitation to prayer. It
invites us to go to the places designated by the Church,
so as to emerge from our everyday routine, from our
self-will into the encounter with God, into the space of
his forgiveness. It invites us to go to the sacrament, because no one can absolve himself. Nowadays there is a
lot of psychoanalysis and psychotherapy, which can help
in many respects. Of course it cannot satisfy the deepest yearning in man: the yearning for absolution. Only
an authority that comes from something greater can bestow that. We are redeemed persons. This very fact also
means that there is an authoritative word of absolution,
of forgiveness. The indulgence invites us to it and to the
sacrament of communion with the Lord and with the
whole Church. And it adds something else: If absolution
is granted to you, then accept the new tune of life, then
let yourself really come around to God's new rhythm!
The first sign of this new tuning of our being is prayer,
for new life means above all else: turning to God. The
indulgenced prayers are, first, the expression of having-
turned-around, of the new direction of our being. Then
they are special prayers in that we let go of these prayers,
as it were, and let them be taken away from us, so to

speak. "Praying for the intention of the Holy Father" means that we place this prayer of ours into the Church's hands. When we do this, we know that, conversely, the whole prayer of the Church belongs to us. As we thus enter into the prayer of the whole Church, we become open to the surplus of good that is in the world, whereas usually we notice first only a surplus of misery, guilt, and evil. By praying our way into this Church, we summon this surplus of good, so that it might cover our weakness, too. This gives us the courage to add our wretched good to it, so that it is in God's hand and will become effective in this world according to his will.

"Now is the acceptable time", we just heard. And we listened to the apostle's appeal: "We beg you on behalf of Christ, be reconciled to God" (2 Cor 5:20). This is the message that the Church wants to announce to us in these days: "Be reconciled with God!" Let us accept this appeal. Let us accept God's Now, and let us pray that our time will not walk right past God's Now, that it will let itself be reconciled, and that the great power of God's reconciliation might produce also the reconciliation with other people for which we are all waiting.

He Restores to Us Our
Dignity as His Children

Josh 5:9a, 10–12; 2 Cor 5:17–21; Lk 15:1–3, 11–32

Dear Brothers and Sisters, dear Boys and Girls,

I have willingly come to pay you a Visit, and the most important moment of our meeting is Holy Mass, where the gift of God's love is renewed: a love that comforts us and gives us peace, especially in life's difficult moments.

In this prayerful atmosphere I would like to address my greeting to each one of you. . . . In the Eucharistic celebration it is Christ himself who becomes present among us; indeed, even more: he comes to enlighten us with his teaching—in the Liturgy of the Word—and to nourish us with his Body and his Blood—in the Eucharistic Liturgy and in Communion.

Thus, he comes to teach us to love, to make us capable of loving and thereby capable of living. But perhaps you will say, how difficult it is to love seriously and to live well! What is the secret of love, the secret of life? Let us return to the Gospel [of the Prodigal Son].

In this Gospel three persons appear: the father and two sons. But these people represent two rather different life projects. Both sons lived peacefully, they were fairly well-off farmers so they had enough to live on, selling their produce profitably, and life seemed good.

Yet little by little the younger son came to find this life boring and unsatisfying: "All of life can't be like this", he thought: rising every day, say at six o'clock, then according to Israel's traditions, there must have been a prayer, a reading from the Holy Bible, then they went to work and at the end of the day another prayer.

Thus, day after day he thought: "But no, life is something more. I must find another life where I am truly free, where I can do what I like; a life free from this discipline, from these norms of God's commandments, from my father's orders; I would like to be on my own and have life with all its beauties totally for myself. Now, instead, it is nothing but work. . . ."

And so he decided to claim the whole of his share of his inheritance and leave. His father was very respectful and generous and respected the son's freedom: it was he who had to find his own life project. And he departed, as the Gospel says, to a far-away country. It was probably geographically distant because he wanted a change, but also inwardly distant because he wanted a completely different life.

So his idea was: freedom, doing what I want to do, not recognizing these laws of a God who is remote, not being in the prison of this domestic discipline, but rather doing what is beautiful, what I like, possessing life with all its beauty and fullness.

And at first—we might imagine, perhaps for a few months—everything went smoothly: he found it beautiful to have attained life at last, he felt happy.

Then, however, little by little, he felt bored here, too; here, too, everything was always the same. And in the end, he was left with an emptiness that was even more disturbing: the feeling that this was still not life became ever more acute; indeed, going ahead with all these things, life drifted farther and farther away. Everything became empty: the slavery of doing the same things then also re-emerged. And in the end, his money ran out, and the young man found that his standard of living was lower than that of swine.

It was then that he began to reflect and wondered if that really was the path to life: a freedom interpreted as doing what I want, living, having life only for me; or if instead it might be more of a life to live for others, to contribute to building the world, to the growth of the human community. . . .

So it was that he set out on a new journey, an inner journey. The boy pondered and considered all these new aspects of the problem and began to see that he had been far freer at home, since he had also been a landowner contributing to building his home and society in communion with the Creator, knowing the purpose of his life and guessing the project that God had in store for him.

During this interior journey, during this development of a new life project and at the same time living the exterior journey, the younger son was motivated to return, to start his life anew because he now understood that he had taken the wrong track. I must start out afresh with a different concept, he said to himself; I must begin again.

And he arrived at the home of the father who had left him his freedom to give him the chance to understand inwardly what life is and what life is not. The father embraced him with all his love, he offered him a feast, and life could start again beginning from this celebration.

The son realized that it is precisely work, humility, and daily discipline that create the true feast and true freedom. So he returned home, inwardly matured and purified: he had understood what living is.

Of course, in the future his life would not be easy, either, temptations would return, but he was henceforth fully aware that life without God does not work; it lacks the essential, it lacks light, it lacks reason, it lacks the great sense of being human. He understood that we can only know God on the basis of his Word.

We Christians can add that we know who God is from Jesus, in whom the face of God has been truly shown to us. The young man understood that God's Commandments are not obstacles to freedom and to a beautiful life, but signposts on the road on which to travel to find life.

He realized, too, that work and the discipline of being committed, not to oneself but to others, extends life. And precisely this effort of dedicating oneself through work gives depth to life, because one experiences the pleasure of having at last made a contribution to the growth of this world that becomes freer and more beautiful.

I do not wish at this point to speak of the other son who stayed at home, but in his reaction of envy we see that inwardly he, too, was dreaming that perhaps it would be far better to take all the freedoms for himself. He, too, in his heart was "returning home" and understanding once again what life is, understanding that it is truly possible to live only with God, with his Word, in the communion of one's own family, of work; in the communion of the great Family of God.

I do not wish to enter into these details now: let each one of us apply this Gospel to himself in his own way. Our situations are different, and each one has his own world. Nonetheless, the fact remains that we are all moved and that we can all enter with our inner journey into the depths of the Gospel.

Only a few more remarks: the Gospel helps us understand who God truly is. He is the Merciful Father who in Jesus loves us beyond all measure.

The errors we commit, even if they are serious, do not corrode the fidelity of his love. In the Sacrament of Confession we can always start out afresh in life. He welcomes us, he restores to us our dignity as his children.

Let us therefore rediscover this sacrament of forgiveness that makes joy well up in a heart reborn to true life.

Furthermore, this parable helps us to understand who the human being is: he is not a "monad", an isolated being who lives only for himself and must have life for himself alone.

On the contrary, we live with others, we were created together with others, and only in being with others, in giving ourselves to others, do we find life.

The human being is a creature in whom God has impressed his own image, a creature who is attracted to the horizon of his Grace, but he is also a frail creature exposed to evil but also capable of good. And lastly, the human being is a free person.

We must understand what freedom is and what is only the appearance of freedom.

Freedom, we can say, is a springboard from which to dive into the infinite sea of divine goodness, but it can also become a tilted plane on which to slide toward the abyss of sin and evil and thus also to lose freedom and our dignity.

Dear friends, we are in the Season of Lent, the forty days before Easter. In this Season of Lent, the Church helps us to make this interior journey and invites us to conversion, which always, even before being an important effort to change our behavior, is an opportunity to decide to get up and set out again, to abandon sin and to choose to return to God.

Let us—this is the imperative of Lent—make this journey of inner liberation together.

Every time, such as today, that we participate in the Eucharist, the source and school of love, we become capable of living this love, of proclaiming it and witnessing to it with our life.

Nevertheless, we need to decide to walk toward Jesus as the Prodigal Son did, returning inwardly and outwardly to his father.

At the same time, we must abandon the selfish attitude of the older son, who was sure of himself, quick to condemn others, and closed in his heart to understanding, acceptance, and forgiveness of his brother, and who forgot that he, too, was in need of forgiveness.

May the Virgin Mary and Saint Joseph, my Patron Saint whose Feast it will be tomorrow, obtain this gift for us; I now invoke him in a special way for each one of you and for your loved ones.

HOLY EUCHARIST

Transformation Occurs in Prayer

Ex 12:1–8, 11–14; 1 Cor 11:23–26; Jn 13:1–15

Dear Brothers and Sisters,

Qui, pridie quam pro nostra omniumque salute pateretur, hoc est hodie, accepit panem: these words we shall pray today in the Canon of the Mass. *"Hoc est hodie"*—the Liturgy of Holy Thursday places the word "today" into the text of the prayer, thereby emphasizing the particular dignity of this day. It was "today" that he did this: he gave himself to us forever in the Sacrament of his Body and Blood. This "today" is first and foremost the memorial of that first Paschal event. Yet it is something more. With the Canon, we enter into this "today". Our today comes into contact with his today. He does this now. With the word "today", the Church's Liturgy wants us to give great inner attention to the mystery of this day, to the words in which it is expressed. We therefore seek to listen in a new way to the institution narrative, in the form in which the Church has formulated it, on the basis of Scripture and in contemplation of the Lord himself.

The first thing to strike us is that the institution narrative is not an independent phrase, but it starts with a relative pronoun: *qui pridie*. This *"qui"* connects the entire narrative to the preceding section of the prayer, "let it become for us the body and blood of Jesus Christ, your only Son, our Lord." In this way, the institution narrative is linked to the preceding prayer, to the entire Canon, and it too becomes a prayer. By no means is it merely an interpolated narrative, nor is it a case of an authoritative self-standing text that actually interrupts the prayer. It *is* a prayer. And only in the course of the prayer is the priestly act of consecration accomplished, which becomes transformation, transubstantiation of our gifts of bread and wine into the Body and Blood of Christ. As she prays at this central moment, the Church is fully in tune with the event that took place in the Upper Room, when Jesus' action is described in the words: *"gratias agens benedixit* —he gave you thanks and praise." In this expression, the Roman liturgy has made two words out of the one Hebrew word *berakha*, which is rendered in Greek with the two terms *eucharistía* and *eulogía*. The Lord gives thanks. When we thank, we acknowledge that a certain thing is a gift that has come from another. The Lord gives thanks and, in so doing, gives back to God the bread, "fruit of the earth and work of human hands", so as to receive it anew from him. Thanksgiving becomes blessing. The offering that we have placed in God's hands returns from him blessed and transformed. The Roman liturgy rightly interprets, therefore, our praying at this sacred moment by means of the words: "through him, we ask you to accept and bless these gifts we offer you in sacrifice." All this lies hidden within the word *"eucharistia"*.

There is another aspect of the institution narrative cited in the Roman Canon on which we should reflect this evening. The praying Church gazes upon the hands and eyes of the Lord. It is as if she wants to observe him, to perceive the form of his praying and acting in that remarkable hour, she wants to encounter the figure of Jesus even, as it were, through the senses. "He took bread in his sacred hands. . . ." Let us look at those hands with which he healed men and women; the hands with which he blessed babies; the hands that he laid upon men; the hands that were nailed to the Cross and that forever bear the stigmata as signs of his readiness to die for love. Now we are commissioned to do what he did: to take bread in our hands so that through the Eucharistic Prayer it will be transformed. At our priestly ordination, our hands were anointed, so that they could become hands of blessing. Let us pray to the Lord at this hour that our hands will serve more and more to bring salvation, to bring blessing, to make his goodness present!

From the introduction to the Priestly Prayer of Jesus (cf. Jn 17:1), the Canon takes these words: "Looking up to heaven, to you his almighty Father. . . ." The Lord teaches us to raise our eyes and, especially, our hearts. He teaches us to fix our gaze upward, detaching it from the things of this world, to direct ourselves in prayer toward God and thus to raise ourselves. In a hymn from the Liturgy of the Hours, we ask the Lord to guard our eyes, so that they do not take in or cause to enter within us *"vanitates"*—vanities, nothings, that which is merely appearance. Let us pray that no evil will enter through our eyes, falsifying and tainting our very being. But we want to pray above all for eyes that see whatever is true,

radiant, and good; so that they become capable of seeing
God's presence in the world. Let us pray that we will
look upon the world with eyes of love, with the eyes of
Jesus, recognizing our brothers and sisters who need our
help, who are awaiting our word and our action.

Having given thanks and praise, the Lord then breaks
the bread and gives it to the disciples. Breaking the bread
is the act of the father of the family who looks after his
children and gives them what they need for life. But it
is also the act of hospitality with which the stranger, the
guest, is received within the family and is given a share
in its life. Dividing (*dividere*), sharing (*condividere*), brings
about unity. Through sharing, communion is created. In
the broken bread, the Lord distributes himself. The gesture of breaking also alludes mysteriously to his death,
to the love that extends even to death. He distributes
himself, the true "bread for the life of the world" (cf.
Jn 6:51). The nourishment that man needs in his deepest self is communion with God himself. Giving thanks
and praise, Jesus transforms the bread; he no longer gives
earthly bread, but communion with himself. This transformation, though, seeks to be the start of the transformation of the world—into a world of resurrection, a world
of God. Yes, it is about transformation—of the new man
and the new world that find their origin in the bread that
is consecrated, transformed, transubstantiated.

We said that breaking the bread is an act of communion, an act of uniting through sharing. Thus, in the act
itself, the intimate nature of the Eucharist is already in-
dicated: it is *agape*, it is love made corporeal. In the word
"*agape*", the meanings of Eucharist and love intertwine.

In Jesus' act of breaking the bread, the love that is shared has attained its most radical form: Jesus allows himself to be broken as living bread. In the bread that is distributed, we recognize the mystery of the grain of wheat that dies and so bears fruit. We recognize the new multiplication of the loaves, which derives from the dying of the grain of wheat and will continue until the end of the world. At the same time, we see that the Eucharist can never be just a liturgical action. It is complete only if the liturgical *agape* then becomes love in daily life. In Christian worship, the two things become one—experiencing the Lord's love in the act of worship and fostering love for one's neighbor. At this hour, we ask the Lord for the grace to learn to live the mystery of the Eucharist ever more deeply, in such a way that the transformation of the world can begin to take place.

After the bread, Jesus takes the chalice of wine. The Roman Canon describes the chalice which the Lord gives to his disciples as *"praeclarus calix"* (the glorious cup), thereby alluding to Psalm 23 [22], the Psalm which speaks of God as the Good Shepherd, the strong Shepherd. There we read these words: "You have prepared a banquet for me in the sight of my foes. . . . My cup is overflowing" —*calix praeclarus*. The Roman Canon interprets this passage from the Psalm as a prophecy that is fulfilled in the Eucharist: yes, the Lord does indeed prepare a banquet for us in the midst of the threats of this world, and he gives us the glorious chalice—the chalice of great joy, of the true feast, for which we all long—the chalice filled with the wine of his love. The chalice signifies the wedding feast: now the "hour" has come to which the wedding feast of Cana had mysteriously alluded. Yes indeed, the Eucharist is more than a meal, it is a wedding feast. And this wedding is rooted in God's gift of himself even to death. In the words of Jesus at the Last Supper and in the Church's Canon, the solemn mystery of the wedding is concealed under the expression "*novum Testamentum*". This chalice is the new Testament—"the new Covenant in my blood", as Saint Paul presents the words of Jesus over the chalice in today's second reading (1 Cor 11:25). The Roman Canon adds: "of the new and everlasting covenant", in order to express the indissolubility of God's nuptial bond with humanity. The reason why older translations of the Bible do not say Covenant, but Testament, lies in the fact that this is no mere contract between two parties on the same level, but it brings into play the infinite distance between God and man. What we call the new and the ancient Covenant is not an agreement between two equal parties, but simply the gift of God who bequeaths to us his love—himself. Certainly, through this gift of his love, he transcends all distance and makes us truly his "partners"—the nuptial mystery of love is accomplished.

In order to understand profoundly what is taking place here, we must pay even greater attention to the words of the Bible and their original meaning. Scholars tell us that in those ancient times of which the histories of Israel's forefathers speak, to "ratify a Covenant" means "to enter with others into a bond based on blood or to welcome the other into one's own covenant fellowship and thus to enter into a communion of mutual rights and obligations". In this way, a real, if non-material, form of consanguinity is established. The partners become in some way "brothers of the same flesh and the same bones". The covenant brings about a fellowship that means peace.[1] Can we now form at least an idea of what happened at the hour of the Last Supper, and what has been renewed ever since, whenever we celebrate the Eucharist? God, the living God, establishes a communion of peace with us, or, to put it more strongly, he creates "consanguinity" between himself and us. Through the Incarnation of Jesus, through the outpouring of his blood, we have been drawn into an utterly real consanguinity with Jesus and thus with God himself. The blood of Jesus is his love, in which divine life and human life have become one. Let us pray to the Lord, that we may come to understand ever more deeply the greatness of this mystery. Let us pray that in our innermost selves its transforming power will increase, so that we truly acquire consanguinity with Jesus, so that we are filled with his peace and grow in communion with one another.

Now, however, a further question arises. In the Upper Room, Christ gives his Body and Blood to the disciples, that is, he gives himself in the totality of his person. But can he do so? He is still physically present in their midst, he is standing in front of them! The answer is: at that hour, Jesus fulfills what he had previously proclaimed in the Good Shepherd discourse: "No one takes my life from me: I lay it down of my own accord. I have power to lay it down and I have power to take it again . . ." (Jn

[1] Cf. *Theologisches Wörterbuch zum Neuen Testament*, ed. Gerhard Kittel et al. (Stuttgart: Kohlhammer, 1933–1979), 2:105–37.

10:18). No one can take his life from him: he lays it down by his own free decision. At that hour, he anticipates the crucifixion and Resurrection. What is later to be fulfilled, as it were, physically in him, he already accomplishes in anticipation, in the freedom of his love. He gives his life and he takes it again in the Resurrection, so as to be able to share it forever.

Lord, today you give us your life, you give us yourself. Enter deeply within us with your love. Make us live in your "today". Make us instruments of your peace!

Amen.

In Bread and Wine He
Gives Himself Entirely

Ex 24:3–8; Heb 9:11–15; Mk 14:12–16, 22–26

Dear Brothers and Sisters,

On the eve of his Passion, during the Passover meal, the Lord took the bread in his hands—as we heard a short time ago in the Gospel passage—and, having blessed it, he broke it and gave it to his Disciples, saying: "Take this, this is my body." He then took the chalice, gave thanks, and passed it to them, and they all drank from it. He said: "This is my blood, the blood of the covenant, to be poured out on behalf of many" (Mk 14:22–24).

The entire history of God with humanity is recapitulated in these words. The past alone is not only referred to and interpreted, but the future is anticipated—the coming of the Kingdom of God into the world. What Jesus says are not simply words. What he says is an event, the central event of the history of the world and of our personal lives.

These words are inexhaustible. In this hour, I would like to meditate with you on just one aspect. Jesus, as a sign of his presence, chose bread and wine. With each one of the two signs he gives himself completely, not only in part. The Risen One is not divided. He is a person who, through signs, comes near to us and unites himself to us. Each sign however, represents in its own way a particular aspect of his mystery and, through its respective manifestation, wishes to speak to us so that we learn to understand the mystery of Jesus Christ a little better.

During the procession and in adoration, we look at the consecrated Host, the most simple type of bread and nourishment, made only of a little flour and water. In this way, it appears as the food of the poor, those to whom the Lord made himself closest in the first place.

The prayer with which the Church, during the liturgy of the Mass, consigns this bread to the Lord, qualifies it as fruit of the earth and the work of humans.

It involves human labor, the daily work of those who till the soil, sow and harvest [the wheat], and, finally, prepare the bread. However, bread is not purely and simply what we produce, something made by us; it is fruit of the earth and therefore is also gift.

We cannot take credit for the fact that the earth produces fruit; the Creator alone could have made it fertile. And now we too can expand a little on this prayer of the Church, saying: the bread is fruit of heaven and earth together. It implies the synergy of the forces of earth and the gifts from above, that is, of the sun and the rain. And water, too, which we need to prepare the bread, cannot be produced by us.

In a period in which desertification is spoken of and where we hear time and again the warning that man and beast risk dying of thirst in these waterless regions—in such a period we realize once again how great is the gift of water and of how we are unable to produce it ourselves. And so, looking closely at this little piece of white Host, this bread of the poor, appears to us as a synthesis of creation. Heaven and earth, too, like the activity and spirit of man, cooperate. The synergy of the forces that make the mystery of life and the existence of man possible on our poor planet come to meet us in all of their majestic grandeur.

In this way, we begin to understand why the Lord chooses this piece of bread to represent him. Creation, with all of its gifts, aspires above and beyond itself to something even greater. Over and above the synthesis of its own forces, above and beyond the synthesis also of nature and of spirit that, in some way, we detect in the piece of bread, creation is projected toward divinization, toward the holy wedding feast, toward unification with the Creator himself.

And still, we have not yet explained in depth the message of this sign of bread. The Lord mentioned its deepest mystery on Palm Sunday, when some Greeks asked to see him. In his answer to this question is the phrase: "Truly, truly, I say to you, unless a grain of wheat falls into the earth and dies, it remains alone; but if it dies, it bears much fruit" (Jn 12:24).

The mystery of the Passion is hidden in the bread made of ground grain. Flour, the ground wheat, presupposes the death and resurrection of the grain. In being ground and baked, it carries in itself once again the same mystery of the Passion. Only through death does resurrection arrive, as does the fruit and new life.

Mediterranean culture, in the centuries before Christ, had a profound intuition of this mystery. Based on the experience of this death and rising, they created myths of divinity which, dying and rising, gave new life. To them, the cycle of nature seemed like a divine promise in the midst of the darkness of suffering and death that we are faced with. In these myths, the soul of the human person, in a certain way, reached out toward that God made man, who, humiliated unto death on a cross, in this way opened the door of life to all of us. In bread and its making, man has understood it as a waiting period of nature, like a promise of nature that this would come to exist: the God that dies and in this way brings us to life.

What was awaited in myths and that in the very grain of wheat is hidden like a sign of the hope of creation—this truly came about in Christ. Through his gratuitous suffering and death, he became bread for all of us and, with this, living and certain hope. He accompanies us in all of our sufferings until death. The paths that he travels with us and through which he leads us to life are pathways of hope.

When, in adoration, we look at the consecrated Host, the sign of creation speaks to us. And so, we encounter the greatness of his gift; but we also encounter the Passion, the Cross of Jesus, and his Resurrection. Through this gaze of adoration, he draws us toward himself, within his mystery, through which he wants to transform us as he transformed the Host.

The primitive Church discovered yet another symbol in the bread. The Doctrine of the Twelve Apostles, a book written around the year 100, contains in its prayers the affirmation: "Even as this broken bread was scattered over the hills, and was gathered together and became one, so let Thy Church be gathered together from the ends of the earth into Thy Kingdom."[1]

Bread made of many grains contains also an event of union: the ground grain becoming bread is a process of unification. We ourselves, many as we are, must become one bread, one body, as Saint Paul says (cf. 1 Cor 10:17). In this way the sign of bread becomes both hope and fulfillment.

In a very similar way, the sign of wine speaks to us. However, while bread speaks of daily life, simplicity, and pilgrimage, wine expresses the exquisiteness of creation: the feast of joy that God wants to offer to us at the end of time and that already now and always anticipates anew a foretaste through this sign.

But, wine also speaks of the Passion: the vine must be repeatedly pruned to be purified in this way; the grapes must mature with the sun and the rain and must be pressed: only through this passion does a fine wine mature.

On the feast of *Corpus Christi*, we especially look at the sign of bread. It reminds us of the pilgrimage of Israel during the forty years in the desert. The Host is our manna whereby the Lord nourishes us—it is truly the bread of heaven, through which he gives himself.

In the procession, we follow this sign, and in this way we follow Christ himself. And we ask of him: Guide us

---

[1] *The Teaching of the Twelve Apostles* IX, 4, in *Ante-Nicene Fathers*, ed. Alexander Roberts and James Donaldson, vol. 7 (1886; Peabody, Mass.: Hendrickson, 1995), 380.

on the paths of our history! Show the Church and her
Pastors again and again the right path! Look at suffering humanity, cautiously seeking a way through so much
doubt; look upon the physical and mental hunger that
torments it! Give men and women bread for body and
soul! Give them work! Give them light! Give them yourself! Purify and sanctify all of us! Make us understand
that only through participation in your Passion, through
"yes" to the cross, to self-denial, to the purifications that
you impose upon us, our lives can mature and arrive at
true fulfillment. Gather us together from all corners of
the earth. Unite your Church, unite wounded humanity!
Give us your salvation! Amen.

ANOINTING OF THE SICK

Living by God's Great Love

Rev 7:2-4, 9-14; Mt 5:1-12

Suppose we went out into the street and asked someone whom he takes as a model and maybe envies a little,
whom he would like to resemble. We would probably
hear the names of some soccer champions, the names of
movie stars or people from show business, maybe the
names of politicians and inventors. The standard behind
this would ultimately be the same one in all cases: being
distinguished and having wealth, power, and health im-
presses people and seems worth striving for.

In the Gospel reading that we just heard, the Lord himself gives an answer to this question and tells us whom
he considers to be the important people, what character-
istics people ought to have in his opinion, the ones about
whom we can say that they are "blessed", that they have it
good, and that it would be worthwhile striving to be like
them. Jesus' answer is diametrically opposed to what they
would tell us on the street and what we ourselves might
say. His standard for being human is expressed in statements like these: "Blessed are the poor in spirit, for theirs

is the kingdom of heaven. Blessed are those who mourn, for they shall be comforted" (Mt 5:3–4). "Blessed are you when men revile you and persecute you and utter all kinds of evil against you falsely on my account. Rejoice and be glad, for your reward is great in heaven" (Mt 5: 11–12).

By this standard, those who suffer are not left behind but are central. Although this standard is so foreign to the natural thinking of people of every era, it nevertheless has not gone without a response. In the reading we heard that in heaven there is a countless multitude of those "who have come out of the great tribulation" (Rev 7:14) and have experienced that what Jesus said is true. By that John means the saints, who in every generation, down through all the centuries, have responded to this standard of Jesus, have translated it into their lives, have given flesh and blood to these words, and have proved that these words are true, this standard is right.

The standard of the saints—these are the Beatitudes from the Sermon on the Mount—is expressed this way in the words of one of the first who followed it, Saint Paul: "I bear on my body the marks of Jesus" (Gal 6:17). And: "in my flesh I complete what is lacking in Christ's afflictions" (Col 1:24). If Jesus Christ is the truly important man, if we become somewhat like him by following him, then we must accept Christ's wounds. The ones who particularly resemble Christ are those who are wounded with him, who bear the marks of his wounds on their bodies, each in his own way. This shows that the wounded, the suffering, are central in God's family. We will understand this more profoundly and also experience more deeply the consolation of Jesus' words if we examine it still more closely with the help of a few examples.

First, let us stay with Saint Paul. He writes to the community in Corinth: "A thorn was given me in the flesh, a messenger of Satan, to harass me, to keep me from being too elated. Three times I begged the Lord about this, that it should leave me; but he said to me, 'My grace is sufficient for you, for my power is made perfect in weakness'" (2 Cor 12:7–9). We do not know what this "thorn in the flesh" was. There are many hypotheses, maybe a serious eye disease, as the Letter to the Galatians seems to hint, or bad rheumatism, constant headaches; some have even mentioned epilepsy. Of one thing we are sure, though: precisely in this human experience of suffering and weakness he experienced the grace and power of God, made it more perceptible, more resonant than others before him had been able to do. While still in prison, he wrote with shackled hands: "Rejoice in the Lord always; again I will say, Rejoice" (Phil 4:4). He had recognized that just so he was very close to the wounded Lord, whose marks he bore, that just so he was especially loved by God, just so he was privileged to learn what is most profound in the human condition more purely than in the superficiality of outward success. And so, too, he not only suffered more, but also did and accomplished more than most healthy people in his century, and he has remained a guide down through the ages.

When we go back to the height of the medieval period, we encounter there the saint who in all of history resembled Christ the most, who was called "the image of

Christ" in the Middle Ages: Francis of Assisi. Before he
received the stigmata, he prayed to Christ: "Grant that I
may learn to love as you loved." He knew that there is
nothing greater, no greater accomplishment, no greater
success, no greater fulfillment of human life than to be
able to love wholly and generously. But as he meditated
more deeply on this request, he was startled and had to
admit that it demanded a second request, which he then
added: "Teach me to suffer as you suffered." For he understood that one can love as Christ did only if one is willing to suffer also as he did. And so he dared to pray for
the wounds of Christ, for the gift of "suffering as Christ
did". These wounds were truly not just a mystical sort of
decoration—in addition, he went noticeably blind. From
contemporary descriptions of his life, we know how ter-
ribly he suffered from the medical arts of that time, when
he was treated without anesthetics with glowing tongs in
order to restore his sight, of course unsuccessfully. And
yet we know that precisely from this little man who suffered so much the great power of love and, consequently,
an important force of gladness also arose. His "Canticle
of the Sun", his praise of the Creator as reflected in creation, resounds through all the centuries. The man who
sang it was not a dreamy troubadour and conservation-
ist, as he is often depicted for us, but rather someone
who accepted sufferings, who wanted to accept them for
Christ's sake, so as to touch with him the depths of the
human condition and the heart of God.

Then at the beginning of the modern era, we meet Saint
Ignatius of Loyola, a soldier and officer, who at first lived
entirely according to the standards about which we spoke

at the beginning, namely, according to the standards of the chivalric romances that were popular at that time, which were all about accomplishing great heroic deeds, making conquests and plundering, having success with women and in politics. One day Ignatius was seriously wounded and now noticed that everything he had viewed as the substance of life, as his ideal and his dream, was really only a dream, something that trickles away and does not last and cannot be the core of reality. He had to look for another, greater reality. So he discovered that there were better wars to wage than the wars in which others are killed, in which they are taken into captivity and robbed of their possessions. He discovered that there are wars of the saints, the campaign of Jesus Christ, which does not aim to kill people but, rather, to reveal to them the true life that does not deprive people of freedom but, rather, brings them real freedom in the first place; which does not plunder but, rather, generously gives; and he found that anyone who acts in this way personally receives life and freedom and grace thereby.

We could continue this way and mention many more names of people who accepted the standard of Jesus Christ, who are not marginal figures but, rather, gave great things and received great things. We could name names down to the present day, for each of us is acquainted with such people, who give us more than we can give them, who bear and endure the human condition more deeply and thereby also do and accomplish more and give us more, because they have descended to a greater depth.

In God's family, there are no marginal figures. This is so because for God, of course, the transient external things do not count; rather, what count are the things that last and are essential: truth and love. No one can love without letting himself be wounded. No one can do the truth without accepting wounds. No one can make peace without exposing himself to wounds. God does not want human suffering. He most certainly does not want it for suffering's sake. But suffering can often be a way by which he comes more profoundly to a person and by which that person comes to him, a way by which such a person then also gives to others what they themselves do not find.

"Rejoice and be glad, for your reward is great in heaven" (Mt 5:12), today's Gospel says. This tells us: Time is transient and insignificant; eternity lasts. Then all our disabilities will be taken from us and all our tears wiped away; then the eyes of the blind and the ears of the deaf shall be opened, and we will behold God's mercies. That is our consolation. But it is not only a prospect of something that will come about someday. The power of God's mercies, the reality of heaven is here even now! Although often it can be recognized only through great obscurity: the Lord is close even now!

Let us pray during this Holy Sacrifice that he will let us sense and experience his closeness again and again in all our afflictions, so that what we heard in the reading can come true: that all who are in great distress might praise God's great glory and that we might be able to live by his love in the hope of faith that he has opened up for us.

Abandoning Oneself
to God's Mercy

Heb 5:7–9; Lk 2:33–35

Dear Brothers in the episcopate and the priesthood, dear
Friends who are sick, dear carers and helpers, dear Brothers and Sisters!

Yesterday we celebrated the Cross of Christ, the instrument of our salvation, which reveals the mercy of our God
in all its fullness. The Cross is truly the place where God's
compassion for our world is perfectly manifested. Today,
as we celebrate the memorial of Our Lady of Sorrows, we
contemplate Mary sharing her Son's compassion for sin-
ners. As Saint Bernard declares, the Mother of Christ entered into the Passion of her Son through her compassion
(cf. *Homily for Sunday in the Octave of the Assumption*). At
the foot of the Cross, the prophecy of Simeon is fulfilled:
her mother's heart is pierced through (cf. Lk 2:35) by the
torment inflicted on the Innocent One born of her flesh.
Just as Jesus cried (cf. Jn 11:35), so too Mary certainly
cried over the tortured body of her Son. Her self-restraint,
however, prevents us from plumbing the depths of her
grief; the full extent of her suffering is merely suggested
by the traditional symbol of the seven swords. As in the
case of her Son Jesus, one might say that she, too, was
led to perfection through this suffering (cf. Heb 2:10),
so as to make her capable of receiving the new spiritual

mission that her Son entrusts to her immediately before "giving up his spirit" (cf. Jn 19:30): that of becoming the Mother of Christ in his members. In that hour, through the figure of the beloved disciple, Jesus presents each of his disciples to his Mother when he says to her: Behold your Son (cf. Jn 19:26–27).

Today Mary dwells in the joy and the glory of the Resurrection. The tears shed at the foot of the Cross have been transformed into a smile which nothing can wipe away, even as her maternal compassion toward us remains unchanged. The intervention of the Virgin Mary in offering succor throughout history testifies to this and does not cease to call forth, in the people of God, an unshakable confidence in her: the *Memorare* prayer expresses this sentiment very well. Mary loves each of her children, giving particular attention to those who, like her Son at the hour of his Passion, are prey to suffering; she loves them quite simply because they are her children, according to the will of Christ on the Cross.

The psalmist, seeing from afar this maternal bond which unites the Mother of Christ with the people of faith, prophesies regarding the Virgin Mary that "the richest of the people . . . will seek your smile" (Ps 44:13).[1] In this way, prompted by the inspired word of Scripture, Christians have always sought the smile of Our Lady, this smile which medieval artists were able to represent with such marvelous skill and to show to advantage. This smile of Mary is for all; but it is directed quite particu-

---

[1] *German:* "will seek your smile"; *Vulgate*: vultum tuum deprecabuntur; *Douay-Rheims:* "will entreat your countenance".

larly to those who suffer, so that they can find comfort
and solace therein. To seek Mary's smile is not an act
of devotional or outmoded sentimentality, but rather the
proper expression of the living and profoundly human
relationship which binds us to her whom Christ gave us
as our Mother.

To wish to contemplate this smile of the Virgin does
not mean letting oneself be led by an uncontrolled imagination. Scripture itself discloses it to us through the lips of
Mary when she sings the Magnificat: "My soul glorifies
the Lord, my spirit exults in God my Savior" (Lk 1:46–
47). When the Virgin Mary gives thanks to the Lord, she
calls us to witness. Mary shares, as if by anticipation, with
us, her future children, the joy that dwells in her heart,
so that it can become ours. Every time we recite the
Magnificat, we become witnesses of her smile. Here in
Lourdes, in the course of the apparition of Wednesday,
March 3, 1858, Bernadette contemplated this smile of
Mary in a most particular way. It was the first response
that the Beautiful Lady gave to the young visionary who
wanted to know who she was. Before introducing herself,
some days later, as "the Immaculate Conception", Mary
first taught Bernadette to know her smile, this being the
most appropriate point of entry into the revelation of her
mystery.

In the smile of the most eminent of all creatures, looking down on us, is reflected our dignity as children of God,
that dignity which never abandons the sick person. This
smile, a true reflection of God's tenderness, is the source
of an invincible hope. Unfortunately we know only too
well: the endurance of suffering can upset life's most

stable equilibrium; it can shake the firmest foundations of confidence, and sometimes even leads people to despair of the meaning and value of life. There are struggles that we cannot sustain alone, without the help of divine grace. When speech can no longer find the right words, the need arises for a loving presence: we seek then the closeness not only of those who share the same blood or are linked to us by friendship, but also the closeness of those who are intimately bound to us by faith. Who could be more intimate to us than Christ and his holy Mother, the Immaculate One? More than any others, they are capable of understanding us and grasping how hard we have to fight against evil and suffering. The Letter to the Hebrews says of Christ that he "is not unable to sympathize with our weaknesses; for in every respect he has been tempted as we are" (cf. Heb 4:15). I would like to say, humbly, to those who suffer and to those who struggle and are tempted to turn their backs on life: turn toward Mary! Within the smile of the Virgin lies mysteriously hidden the strength to fight against sickness and for life. With her, equally, is found the grace to accept without fear or bitterness to leave this world at the hour chosen by God.

How true was the insight of that great French spiritual writer, Dom Jean-Baptiste Chautard, who in *L'âme de tout apostolat*, proposed to the devout Christian to gaze frequently "into the eyes of the Virgin Mary"! Yes, to seek the smile of the Virgin Mary is not a pious infantilism, it is the aspiration, as Psalm 44 says, of those who are "the richest of the people" (verse 13). "The richest", that is to say, in the order of faith, those who have attained the highest degree of spiritual maturity and know precisely how to acknowledge their weakness and their poverty before God. In the very simple manifestation of tenderness that we call a smile, we grasp that our sole wealth is the love God bears us, which passes through the heart of her who became our Mother. To seek this smile is first of all to have grasped the gratuitousness of love; it is also to be able to elicit this smile through our efforts to live according to the word of her Beloved Son, just as a child seeks to elicit its mother's smile by doing what pleases her. And we know what pleases Mary, thanks to the words she spoke to the servants at Cana: "Do whatever he tells you" (cf. Jn 2:5).

Mary's smile is a spring of living water. "He who believes in me", says Jesus, "out of his heart shall flow rivers of living water" (Jn 7:38). Mary is the one who believed, and, from her womb, rivers of living water have flowed forth to irrigate human history. The spring that Mary pointed out to Bernadette here in Lourdes is the humble sign of this spiritual reality. From her believing heart, from her maternal heart, flows living water which purifies and heals. By immersing themselves in the baths at Lourdes, so many people have discovered and experienced the gentle maternal love of the Virgin Mary, becoming attached to her in order to bind themselves more closely to the Lord! In the liturgical sequence of this feast of Our Lady of Sorrows, Mary is honored with the title of *Fons amoris*, "fount of love". From Mary's heart, there springs up a gratuitous love which calls forth a response of filial love, called to ever greater refinement. Like every mother, and better than every mother, Mary is the teacher of love. That is why so many sick people come here to Lourdes, to quench their thirst at the "spring of love" and to let themselves be led to the sole source of salvation, her son, Jesus the Savior.

Christ imparts his salvation by means of the sacraments and, especially in the case of those suffering from sickness or disability, by means of the grace of the Sacrament of the Sick. For each individual, suffering is always something alien. It can never be tamed. That is why it is hard to bear, and harder still—as certain great witnesses of Christ's holiness have done—to welcome it as a significant element in our vocation, or to accept, as Bernadette expressed it, to "suffer everything in silence in order to please Jesus". To be able to say that, it is necessary to have traveled a long way already in union with Jesus. Here and now, though, it is possible to entrust oneself to God's mercy, as manifested through the grace of the Sacrament of the Sick. Bernadette herself, in the course of a life that was often marked by sickness, received this sacrament four times. The grace of this sacrament consists in welcoming Christ the healer into ourselves. However, Christ is not a healer in the manner of the world. In order to heal us, he does not remain outside the suffering that is experienced; he eases it by coming to dwell within the one stricken by illness, to bear it and live it with him. Christ's presence comes to break the isolation which pain induces. Man no longer bears his burden alone: as a suffering member of Christ, he is conformed to Christ in his self-offering to the Father, and he participates, in him, in the coming to birth of the new creation.

Without the Lord's help, the yoke of sickness and suffering weighs down on us cruelly. By receiving the Sacrament of the Sick, we seek to carry no other yoke than that of Christ, strengthened through his promise to us that his yoke will be easy to carry and his burden light (cf. Mt 11:30). I invite those who are to receive the Sacrament of the Sick during this Mass to enter into a hope of this kind.

The Second Vatican Council presented Mary as the figure in whom the entire mystery of the Church is typified (cf. *Lumen gentium*, 63–65). Her personal journey outlines the profile of the Church, which is called to be just as attentive to those who suffer as she herself was. I extend an affectionate greeting to those working in the areas of public health and nursing as well as those who, in different ways, in hospitals and other institutions, are contributing to the care of the sick with competence and generosity. Equally, I should like to say to all the *hospitaliers*, the *brancardiers*, and the carers who come from every diocese in France and from farther afield, and who throughout the year attend the sick who come on pilgrimage to Lourdes, how much their service is appreciated. They are the arms of the servant Church. Finally, I wish to encourage those who, in the name of their faith, receive and visit the sick, especially in hospital infirmaries, in parishes or, as here, at shrines. May you always sense in this important and delicate mission the effective and fraternal support of your communities! In this regard, I particularly greet and thank my brothers in the Episcopate, the French bishops, bishops and priests from afar, and all who serve the sick and suffering throughout the world. Thank you for your ministry close to our suffering Lord.

The service of charity that you offer is a Marian service. Mary entrusts her smile to you, so that you yourselves may become, in faithfulness to her son, springs of living water. Whatever you do, you do in the name of the Church, of which Mary is the purest image. May you carry her smile to everyone!

To conclude, I wish to join in the prayer of the pilgrims and the sick, and to pray with you a passage from the prayer to Mary that has been proposed for this Jubilee celebration:

"Because you are the smile of God, the reflection of the light of Christ, the dwelling place of the Holy Spirit,

Because you chose Bernadette in her lowliness, because you are the morning star, the gate of heaven, and the first creature to experience the resurrection,

Our Lady of Lourdes", with our brothers and sisters whose hearts and bodies are in pain, we pray to you!

MATRIMONY

Maturing in Love

1 Cor 12:31—13:13, Jn 2:1-11

The theologians of the Middle Ages taught us that marriage is the oldest, the first sacrament. God instituted it on the morning of creation, when he created mankind as man and woman, when he gave them to each other as contrasting and complementary companions and helpmates.

This sacrament was created along with creation itself; its significance is interpreted in the prophetically inspired word that the Bible places on Adam's lips in the creation account: "A man leaves his father and his mother and clings to his wife, and they become one flesh" (Gen 2:24). "To cling" is a word that is used in the Bible also for man's relation to God. It expresses a togetherness in which the individual steps outside of himself and gives himself over to the other, so that I and Thou merge, and now neither can be thought of apart from the other; they belong to each other so thoroughly that the future of each is given to the other, too.

From this perspective, we understand also the biblical formula: "They become one flesh." This is not something merely biological; rather, for the Bible, man is an indivisible whole, and "being one flesh" means a new existence with one another in which I and Thou are certainly not dissolved, yet in this "clinging", in this togetherness, a new unity comes about, a unity created by love that gives us some sense of the mystery of the Triune God.

This co-existence and pro-existence that Adam's words designate as "one flesh" are a sacrament, though. This means that not only do we find here two people together, but God is in it with them, for a sacrament is by its nature a way in which God the Invisible comes to us through visible things, in which something visible that belongs to this world becomes a path on which he comes to meet us, on which we, as it were, can touch and experience him.

So we can say that marriage is the oldest, the first, and original way in which God shows himself to man and makes possible a relation with him. Through the other spouse, something of the Lord is supposed to appear, and, conversely, we should always try also to see the other from God's perspective and to see behind the spouse, precisely through what is human, the One who created and loves and accompanies him. Thus, in the goodness of the other spouse, something of the goodness of our life itself should shine forth, and we should recognize that it is good to be a human being, that the world is good, that it is not mere chance but, rather, comes from a goodness that is greater than what we can do and imagine. This definition of God in terms of creation, this sacrament of creation, may have been obscured over the course of history, but it could not be abolished. This commission remains the central core, although of course we must also add that nowhere does creation stand before us as pure and original as it came from God's hands, because meanwhile there has been history and man has added his own contribution to it, part of which is always failure and guilt. So it happens that marriage is not only togetherness in the joy of the mutually experienced goodness, but this encounter always means hardship also and becomes a limit on me, that I experience the difference of the other spouse as disturbing, that I sometimes see the spouse's mistakes more than his good deeds, and on all sides, again, failure and guilt are always there.

But precisely in this way, marriage can become a sacrament once again and more deeply. For only in the willingness to begin again constantly, in the ability to be magnanimous over and over and to see and recognize the original goodness, in a willingness to forgive and to put up with faults, does true, great, mature love grow. Only therein does a person himself become broadminded and mature, pure and great. What was promise and expectation in the beginning becomes whole only in the purifications of daily patience.

And in this way everyday life in itself serves the cause of love, everyday routine serves the marital communion of the image and likeness of God, its growth in us. For, indeed, God himself also entered a covenant with man, which the Bible describes as a sort of marriage, and in this togetherness with mankind, he must again and again tolerate the degree to which it falls short of his love. But he does not fall short. He always comes anew, and about this there are moving, beautiful words, when God says to Israel: I will go out to you in the desert. I will speak to you as in the days of your youth. "I have loved you with an everlasting love; therefore I have continued my faithfulness to you" (Jer 31:3).

All this is sacrament and is included in this gift of God. The reading from the First Letter to the Corinthians just described for us the meaning of this love that matures only in the patience of togetherness. It entails more than the grand momentary gesture; it involves patience (1 Cor 13:4a) and magnanimity, which are also capable of over-looking something and forgetting it; it involves kindness (1 Cor 13:4b) and a good sense of humor; it includes trust and overcoming jealousy. It is important not to put oneself forward and, so to speak, take up all the space for oneself (1 Cor 13:4c). It also means self-control and moderation, which involves not bearing grudges (1 Cor 13:5), not gloating when the other person is wrong but rather rejoicing in what is good. Thus, in trust, in hope, in "standing by" each other together, love grows and extends into the eternity that "never ends" (1 Cor 13:7–8).

Once again we come back to the beginning. We said that marriage is a sacrament given by the Creator, a kind of togetherness in which he himself is present and consequently also opens up the sacred space in which new human life can grow and mature. This space has become distorted in history, but never has the Creator's will been completely destroyed. We can add here that in all peoples and in all historical cultures, it has been known that something sacred is at work in the togetherness of man and woman, that sacred ground (so to speak) is being trod-

den upon, that this togetherness can be successful only
when it occurs in coexistence with God. The fact that
it has a sacred character means that in all cultures it is
something like a sacrament. Now, of course, the image
of God has been distorted and displaced, along with the
standards that men have derived from it. And this is why
it was important, necessary, for God to remove the am-
biguity, to show who he is and to become one of us in
Jesus Christ.

However, because one and the same God is the Creator and the Redeemer, the sacrament of the Creator
is also a sacrament of Jesus Christ, a sacrament of the
New Covenant. It does not remain behind in the merely
natural, pre-Christian realm but, rather, enters into this
covenant, also. In a wedding and in marriage, as the
Gospel says, Christ is present, too (Jn 2:2). This Gospel
passage in its profound symbolic language movingly depicts the interpenetration of creation and sacrament, of
Old and New Covenant, of human love and divine favor.
But I do not wish to explain all this further here—just a
few small suggestions at the conclusion.

The important thing is that Jesus is there and the disciples are there with him. He never comes alone. He comes
in the company of the disciples, and we find him there
again and again. This is why it is important for the sacrament, for its success and persistence, to be with his disciples and to find there the togetherness that we need.
And what John says right at the start is important, too:
Mary "was there" (Jn 2:1). If we read the Gospel and
meditate a little, we see that in her womanly discretion,
in her kind regard, she actually holds the whole thing

together and turns it the right way. And it is as though the Lord wanted to tell us, to tell you, through this Gospel passage: Let the Mother of Jesus be there with you. He gave her to us so that she can help. She does not abandon us, and she leads us again and again to the Lord.

And then, finally, there is this remarkable story about the two wines, the second of which is the better one, to the amazement of the experienced chief steward and contrary to his previous experiences. In the language of the Bible, wine is an image for love. The first wine is young love, the early-morning mutual encounter, the dawn of joy in each other, the gift of creation that was never snuffed out and for which we should be thankful with great joy—and are, too, in this hour. But if we kept relying only on ourselves, if two people relied only on each other, then probably the wine would become scarce, or only water would be left, and what began as a great hope would turn into disappointments and discontent. Or the wine might go bad and taste like vinegar: nothing but the bitterness of daily drudgery might be perceived, and the joy of the great beginning might be forgotten.

The Gospel tells us, though: If we live with the Lord, when this togetherness is started over again and again based on this sacrament, when this getting along with each other and forgiveness occur from this perspective, as Saint Paul says, then water is transformed into wine. Then, for the first time in these transformations, the great wine matures that, contrary to all worldly experience, is even better and nobler than the first, because only now has it reached the full maturity of a time-tested life and a oneness in their being-together with Christ.

Only the second wine, so to speak, gives a full taste of God's goodness and makes us know already in the midst of this age who he is and how good he is.

Dear Newlyweds, in this hour we rejoice with you, that he willed to give you this wine with his promise. We wish for you that the Lord and his disciples and Mary will be "there" in communion with you and that from there he will again and again give the transforming power that changes water into the wine of love, into the wine of his holy sacrament, and that this togetherness may thus really be and remain a gift from him, in which he allows you to experience his goodness.

To Love Means to Give Oneself

Eph 5:21–33

At the start of your wedding day and of the Sacrament of Matrimony that you administer to each other stands Saint John the Baptist. He leads and accompanies you into this sacrament.

He calls himself "the friend of the Bridegroom" (Jn 3:29). Therefore, he is interpreting the mystery of Christ as a nuptial mystery. The Lord came in order to invite people to God's great wedding feast, and he not only invited them to it but also inaugurated it. The Son of God took on human nature and thus intended to draw the whole man, mankind, all people to himself. And through man he united all of creation with God, so that creation and Creator become one and God is "all in all" (1 Cor 15:28, Douay-Rheims). This is the great wedding that consists of the Incarnation of Jesus Christ, his life, his death, and his Resurrection.

The Lord himself is the Bridegroom. This wedding is not a process of nature, not an ascent of evolution, as some imagine it, in which creation slowly ascends to God by itself. It is a process of love, because God himself is a person. Therefore this wedding, this unification of creation and Creator, can occur only in a personal way, in an act of love. This happens through the self-abandonment of the Son, through the fact that he becomes a gift and sacrifices himself entirely for us, and only in this way do we become capable of being with him. Thus the mystery of Christ also sheds light on what the Sacrament of Matrimony is. It represents something that happens on a higher level in his Incarnation.

Saint Paul explained this quite concretely in the second reading that we just heard. He quotes the words that are placed on Adam's lips in the Book of Genesis, at the beginning of creation: "For this reason a man shall leave his father and mother and be joined to his wife, and the two shall become one flesh" (Eph 5:31)—a unique, new communion in Christ, an inseparable, unchangeable, and indestructible unity according to the Creator's will.

The theologians of the Middle Ages understood these words of Adam as a prophecy that was placed on his lips by the Holy Spirit. They found in it an expression of the fact that marriage is a sacrament of creation, instituted by the Creator himself along with creation even before the Fall. It is part of the nature of creation, the nature of mankind, of man and woman. Man is willed by the Creator as a relational being, as someone who is not sufficient unto himself but, rather, needs relationship, who is supposed to live with another and for another. Only in this relatedness to the other and for the other can he fulfill God's will.

And marriage, the mutuality of husband and wife, is the most profound expression, the centerpiece of this relatedness in which man's nature consists. Therefore, the most profound pro-existence of husband and wife, which constitutes man's nature, is love as an act of self-giving. Love is not just a mood or a beautiful feeling. Love makes demands on the whole person. Love means precisely this not-being-for-oneself but, rather, being-for-the-other. It means giving oneself to another as a gift. The Lord set for us an example of what love is when he gave himself as a sacrifice.

Love means giving oneself, living entirely for the other, and that is at the same time the innermost core of marriage.

Thus we see that the sacrament of creation that belongs to the creaturely essence of man already bears within itself the sign of Jesus Christ; that the mystery of Christ is already sketched in creatures and in the midst of creation, in the mutuality and pro-existence of husband and wife.

And we see that creation is on the way toward the mystery of Christ and that thereby the sacrament of creation, marriage, is intrinsically on the way to being the sacrament of Christ and in fact becomes his sacrament and thus takes on its fullness at the moment when he establishes the New Covenant through his sacrifice and fulfills what creation is expecting.

Christ himself gives himself to us and shows us what it means to follow him and to imitate him by giving him to each other. The innermost mystery of Christ is, therefore, reflected in marriage. In its greatness we can see it at this hour, but it must also be translated into the littleness of everyday routine, into constant readiness to start again, to give oneself, to follow Christ, and thus to perfect creation.

In this imitation of God, in being with Christ, a great thing happens: man is privileged to be God's co-creator in creation. Children are, on the one hand, truly new creations from God's hand—only God can create new life

—but they are also your children, children of mankind. Here we can find the intimate intertwining of God and man, the combined effect of God and man in the mystery of creation, with Christ, on which the greatness of creation itself is imprinted.

This is the magnificent aspect of your promise. For giving children to each other means not only that you give them to each other, but also that you give them to God, so that they themselves might become bearers of the mystery of Christ, in that you give them yourselves, your time, your being.

In a wedding, the fundamental formula of human existence is manifested, which Christ gave us: "Whoever seeks to gain his life will lose it, but whoever loses his life will preserve it" (Lk 17:33).

At this point, I would like also to select from the wealth of today's readings a point on which we might want to contradict Saint Paul. Paul begins by saying what we gladly accept: "Be subject to one another out of reverence for Christ" (Eph 5:21). Then he continues: "Wives, be subject to your husbands, . . . as the Church is subject to Christ" (Eph 5:22, 24). "For the husband is the head of the wife as Christ is the head of the Church" (Eph 5:23). Here we would like to object and ask Paul whether he is really right. Paul seems to argue on the basis of his era, but we live today in another era! It is true that a particular sociological understanding is expressed in these verses. But when we study the text thoroughly, we will see that Paul is saying something to us that is new and truly revolutionary for every era, the newness that Jesus Christ brought to us.

How did Jesus Christ show that he is the head, that he

is the Lord, the only and supreme Lord? He showed us this by becoming the last one, by putting himself in the last place, by becoming the servant of us all, by performing for his own disciples the lowly service of a slave and washing their feet. Christ has proclaimed his headship to his disciples and interpreted it by saying: "The Son of man also came not to be served but to serve, and to give his life as a ransom for many" (Mk 10:45). This is Christ's way of being the first, and the husband understands it when he imitates Christ and sees his greatness in the dynamic act of being subordinate to the other.

Everything is renewed through Christ's example. This means that husband and wife imitate this example and grow toward each other by striving not to be served but rather to serve.

Saint Paul explains this in a different way with the statements: Christ "cleansed" the Church, and he "nourishes" her (see Eph 5:26, 29).

Over and over again, he practices this cleansing in his forgiveness. The act of giving is always forgiveness, too, a willingness to start over and to let love begin anew by the power of forgiveness. This happens when we pray together and listen to the word of Scripture so as to be healed ourselves by the word of the Lord; when we receive the Sacrament of Penance and begin again and, thus, receive this gift of continuous renewal and sanctification in which love grows and the process of becoming one flesh and one spirit increasingly becomes a reality.

And Christ nourishes the Church. This is very concrete for a husband and wife in their care for their daily sustenance. It concerns, on the one hand, the Christian household and Christian marriage and, on the other hand, the liturgy and God's house. The connection between the two is very close. Paul says that the two belong together. The life of the family's house depends on the life of the larger house, the Church. And only in a person who lives in God's great house, and in the communion of the liturgy and the sacraments in which Christ "nourishes", can the sacrament become real in his everyday routine and in himself.

But the converse is also true: the house of the Church and the great gift of the Lord's presence in it can become real and concrete only if this gift is taken out into the house of life, if it is endured, prayed, and preserved there. This is Christ's sacrament, which permeates all of life and unites it with himself.

That is my wish for your marriage: that the interpenetration of the mystery of Christ and of creation may make your human love grow more and more and that the joy of the nuptial mystery may always be in you.

HOLY ORDERS

Follow—Leave—Proclaim

1 Cor 2:1–9; Lk 9:57–62

The real event in priestly ordination occurs in the silence during the imposition of hands. With this gesture, the Lord reaches for you, so to speak, my dear friends; he accepts your willingness, which you have just expressed. It is as though he said to you: "You are mine now. Your ways are to be my ways. You are to be a voice for me in this world and an instrument, to such an extent that you are privileged to speak in my person, with my 'I': 'This is my body.' 'I forgive you your sins.'"

Thus this little gesture contains everything that priestly ordination is. In it there is a wordless explanation of the whole event that we now may find again in reverse order in the Gospel passage that we just heard with its three imperatives, which in Holy Orders become Christ's present speech to you: "Follow—leave—proclaim!" (Lk 9:59–60). Accordingly, let us listen a bit more closely to these three calls, in order to understand better what the Lord wants of you—of us.

To impose hands is to take possession. Its purpose is
to make over one's own being to another person, to the
Other: Christ. It is to be dispossessed of one's own being
for his benefit. Now I no longer simply belong to myself and can no longer say: I am I, my life belongs to me
alone, and I will do with it whatever I want. No, what is
true now is the model that Christ placed before us as the
manner of his own being: "My teaching is not mine" (Jn
7:16). I am not mine, but his. My life from now on is
always coexistence with him: living, thinking, doing, and
going with him. I myself do not devise the plan of my
life or the projects of my life but, rather, receive them in
being with him. Thus, the first thing in priestly life is this
opening of my I, the subordination of it to his Thou. It is
basically communion with Jesus, listening to him, living
within reach of him, within the reach of his view and
his voice. Priestly life can succeed and become mature
and fruitful only if this inmost core is not lacking, if it
is always fed by this basis, by participation in his being.
Only from this interior life together with him can collaboration grow, an action that comes from him and leads to
him. Let us pray in harmony to God for this today: that
your lives may always move within the reach of his voice
and his view; that you may become acquainted with Jesus
from within and, thus, become first-hand believers, who
proclaim him to whom you are interiorly close.

Saint Paul, in his Letter to Timothy, summarizes this
core of discipleship in a word when he addresses Timothy as "man of God" (1 Tim 6:11). By this he means
priesthood: the fact that a man becomes a "godly man".
Paul took this title from the Old Testament, where it is a

name for Moses and the prophets—those, therefore, who
brought the unknown, inaccessible, and distant God into
this world, so that he became close and known. More
important than all the other actions of priestly ministry,
however meaningful they may be, is this: that a man himself is touched by God and makes him tangible for others. Precisely in the profane, godforsaken world of today,
people are quietly waiting for there to be men of God
through whom something of God's light becomes perceptible among us. When Moses came down from the
mountain, his face shone (Ex 34:29). People should notice about the priest that he comes again and again from
the mountain of encounters: that the light of Christ has
fallen on him.

So the first call, "follow", leads us automatically to
the second: "leave", There is no following, no walk with
Jesus, without sacrifice, without giving up oneself, without walking away from oneself. Saint Paul emphasizes in
today's reading what this leaving meant in practice for
him: "I did not come proclaiming to you the testimony
of God in lofty words of wisdom. For I decided to know
nothing among you except Jesus Christ and him crucified" (1 Cor 2:1–2). In this twofold "not" of today's
reading, we can see renunciation, the radical change in
his life that became his path in the hour of Damascus.
Now he no longer pursued *his* career or did *his* work,
whereby the great ones build a monument for *themselves*
in the world. Now his purpose of being on the road is to
make the other—Christ—audible. This is the new and
different greatness of the apostle: that he does not seek his
own greatness but, rather, that the Lord's greatness may

be recognized through him. We must attempt this abandonment. The priest is not there to present himself and to create a great impression of himself. He does not proclaim what he himself has thought up, does not seek his own ingenuity. He speaks the word of another and makes over to him his own thoughts and words. He should become as clearly audible as possible, without distortion.

This demands a discipline that encompasses all of life. We do not proclaim ourselves, but Christ. One can attain this discipline, which always measures thinking and speaking in terms of him, only if one's entire life-style bows to the call: "leave". Then one cannot live as though nothing else had changed. "Leave the dead to bury their own dead", the Lord says in the Gospel (Lk 9:60a). By the dead, he means the whole realm of the dead and, therefore, especially attachment to what is dead, to the "things" that I possess and that immediately own me and bind me to what is dead and transient. Even though we cannot all become Francis of Assisi, it is nevertheless true for us all that some degree of simplicity and freedom with regard to external things must grow, so that we attain that interior freedom which is necessary for our ministry.

"Leave!" That means, therefore, the self-control and discipline in our lives by which we are weaned from our own will and conformed to his. It also means the courage to accept the pain of purifications that God imposes on us, because only through the pain of purifications can fruitfulness come about. In every age, the Church can be a mother and become fruitful only if she accepts the pain of transformation, of new birth.

This recalls a prayer of the Curé of Ars, which is moving precisely in its unsentimental simplicity. He said to the Lord: "I love you, my Lord and Master, because you allowed yourself to be crucified for me. I love you, because you consider me crucified for you." Only in this sort of participation in the pain of transformation, in the willingness to be weaned from our own will and conformed to his will, does new life come about, just as the Church came about not only through the word of Jesus but, ultimately, because he fell silent in his Passion and death. It was no different along the road of the Apostle Paul, and in all generations it can be no different.

With that we have arrived again at the call to discipleship, for following Jesus Christ does not mean imitating him in one thing or another, adopting this or that point in a program. Discipleship means following after *him*, taking as our way *Christ himself*, who is the pass-over, the Paschal transformation.

And so this brings us now to the third imperative in today's Gospel. "Proclaim the kingdom of God", the Lord says to the young man (Lk 9:60b). This means: proclaim that God reigns! Proclaim that God is God, that he exists, and that he is God down into the concrete things of our life! Let God be present in his divinity, in his rule, which is our only home! Paul emphasizes this in the reading when he says: "[We proclaim] what no eye has seen, nor ear heard" (1 Cor 2:9). The messenger of Jesus must lead people to what cannot be seen immediately and yet is the essential thing. He must bring God's love into the hearts of people, so that in this way their eyes, too, might see. Again and again the priest must lead the people to recognize that the tangible things that seem to us to be all that is real are not the most reliable and substantial reality, since the true foundation of all things is precisely what cannot be grasped: the living God. Only in such a conversion, in such a transformation of the standpoint of our existence, do we receive what truly lasts, become godly people, and experience what the Lord has prepared for us.

"Proclaim the kingdom of God!" The Holy Father in one of his Holy Thursday letters about the Curé of Ars outlined the mission of the priest in three steps: Proclamation of the faith, purification of conscience, Eucharist. What Jesus' call to proclaim the reign of God means is translated by these key words into the practice of the priestly life. Let us look even more closely at these three areas.

First there is the mission of proclaiming the faith. To proclaim the faith means to place its reality in front of the people and not to drown it in our erudite considerations or explanations. Paul emphasizes this repeatedly in his letter, in today's reading as also in the First Letter to the Thessalonians with his renunciation of the rhetoric of his day and its art of persuasion (1 Thess 2:1–12). We need again the courage to call the simple reality of the faith into this world straightforwardly and without excuses. Only when this happens, only when the living God dawns in the hearts of men, does the purification of consciences come to pass.

And the real burden of our time is, after all, precisely this silencing of the conscience. When we think of what drug dealers, arms traffickers, and all sorts of oppressors can do—what trampling on conscience! When sin is still known as sin, the pathway to healing is still open. The sickness of souls becomes truly life-threatening when the conscience no longer speaks and sin is no longer recognized and acknowledged as sin.

The Curé of Ars once said to his parishioners: "I weep over the fact that you do not weep over your sins." The consequence of this insensibility to our divine calling—of this silencing of the conscience—is that the deepest part of man, which is his real dignity, does not awaken. This calls to mind a remark by Gregory the Great, who in his Homilies on Ezekiel once said that in order to become an evangelist, someone must become like a human being, but that we become human only if we become like Christ. The purification of conscience is what makes the heart open and wide; this is what gives us access to the mystery of the Eucharist, to the presence of God's love in the midst of this world of ours.

Dear friends, this is the mission that you receive in this hour, the mission contained in the imposition of hands. Although all this may perhaps seem to us too great for our capacities, you should reflect that the imposition of hands is not only an act of taking possession but at the same time a gesture of kindness, tenderness, protection. Through it the Lord says not only: "You are mine", but also: "I want to be yours and to accompany you on all your paths. Wherever you walk, you go in the shadow of my hands."

Therefore, we pray for you in this hour, that you will walk on all your paths in the shadow of his blessing hands and that this blessing will pass on from you to the people whom the Lord entrusts to you.

I No Longer Call You
Servants, but Friends

Jer 1:4–10; 2 Cor 1:18, 22–24; Jn 15:9–17

The first sentence of today's Gospel is of such magnitude that it would actually overwhelm us if we were not dulled by familiarity with it. "As the Father has loved me, so have I loved you" (Jn 15:9), says the Lord. This means: with the same love with which God loves himself, with the same love with which the Son is devoted to his Father— with that same love, the Lord loves us. We are known, we are loved, we are accepted. Our existence in the world is not empty; we are not cast into a meaningless darkness without knowing whence it comes or whither it leads. An indestructible love accepted us in advance and goes with us.

We are loved. This means: we are needed. For someone who is loved is needed, is necessary for the one who loves him. God, who is in need of no one, loves us, and so the improbable fact is true: he needs us, we have become necessary for him. We are needed. We are not without purpose in the world. He wants us. He is in need of us.

This being-needed, which gives our life meaning, becomes concrete in a special way in the priesthood. What Jesus said to his disciples applies to priests in a peculiar way: "I chose you and appointed you that you should go and bear fruit and that your fruit should abide" (Jn

15:16). The Lord needs us to "go and bear fruit". He went forth from the eternal glory of God in order to bring us God's Yes, to show us the way, to be the Way for us. He wants us to continue this going-forth of God, and this is exactly his will for the priest specifically. That we set out for him and go on our way, so that he can keep coming to man. He wants you to bear fruit along that way.

This echoes again the preceding metaphor of the grape-vine (Jn 15:1–8). The Lord tells us: In tending a grapevine, it is important not to let the leaves grow too luxuriantly; it has to be cut back, so that finally the branches are not bare and useless but, instead, fruit grows. Part of bearing fruit is being purified, being cut back again and again, which takes away from us leaves and unnecessary twigs that serve no purpose. It requires the patience of maturation and of being cleansed; the humility to accept this cleansing from God and to recognize his kind hand in it. In order for there to be fruit, in order for delicious wine to be made from the grapes, it requires sunlight, but also the storm, both the dark and the light. All this is found in our lives, and not by accident. We know that the Lord helps us to bring forth fruit.

But what is meant by: "fruit should abide" (Jn 15:16)? Everyone knows that he does not simply go away from the world without a trace when he must die. Ingrained in everyone is this silent rebellion against death. We want to leave something of ourselves behind, to carve some sign onto the field of history. In this way, based on this intention to bring forth something lasting and not simply to disappear with one's life into nothingness, great and terrible political deeds have been born. From it art and science have developed, in which man tries to bring forth fruit and wishes not only to know but also somehow personally to abide.

Much can come about in this way, and nevertheless everything we do, even if it lasts far beyond our lifetime, is subject to transience. Buildings collapse, books that are supposed to provide eternity pass away, and often such self-made eternity can be very short-lived. What remains? The only immortal thing is the human heart, and fruit that lasts is therefore only what we were able to give to a person so that it helped him to live. Fruit that lasts is what has sunk into a human heart so that it became part of himself and of his eternity. Fruit that lasts is the light that we have instilled in people by a word of faith, by a deed done out of love, by serving in the spirit of the Lord, by giving ourselves away. And then, of course, something great and astonishing happens: God expects this fruit that he himself cannot create, which comes only from human freedom. Let us pray to the Lord that you may bring forth a great harvest of everlasting fruit in this way as servants of God's joy.

Out of the great wealth of today's Scripture passages I would like to single out one more message, a statement that has accompanied me since my own priestly ordination: "No longer do I call you servants . . . but . . . friends" (Jn 15:15). At that time it was the verse with which the ceremony of priestly ordination ended, which, so to speak, was to open the door leading to everyday life: Go out into the Lord's friendship, knowing that he goes with you as a friend. Often we think: This creature, man, is after all so small in the universe; it is absolutely impossible for God to know us individually, to take an interest in us. But no: he has made us servants into friends.

But of what does this friendship consist? How is it lived out in practice? The Lord gives us two answers to this question. The first: "You are my friends if you do what I command you" (Jn 15:14). That is not an egotistical condition, whereby the Lord was saying something like: "If you dance to the tune that I pipe, then you are my friends." It is something else entirely. Hidden behind it is the deepest nature of all friendship, which the ancient Romans defined by the saying: *idem velle, idem nolle*—to want the same thing and not to want the same thing. A communion of will, agreement about what one most profoundly wishes. Friendship with Christ, therefore, means that the two wills, his and ours, become one. He preceded us, he placed his will in ours, so much so that he left his divinity behind, set aside his glory, and became man with us (Phil 2:6–7). That is how much he has taken to heart our will to be right, to be happy. This is how much this will of ours has become his: for its sake, he laid down his life as a true friend: "Greater love has no man than this, that a man lay down his life for his friends" (Jn 15:13). He made our will his and gave his own away.

So he invites us in turn to enter into his will, which in advance harmonizes with our deepest, true will. He invites us to do what he did. He invites us no longer to look after ourselves constantly, no longer to be determined to get what I would like, so that we are trapped in perpetual worry and can never be satisfied. He tells us: Leave, then, your will and your worries to me; I already care for you. We can leave our will to him. There it will be kept safely. The Lord is not forgetful, and he is not weak, he is not unreliable. With assurance we can deposit our will with him and thus become tranquil and free and, instead, try to accept his will, the most important thing in this world. His will, though, is that people might know God, that they learn to live righteously, that they become one in their faith in God. This venturing into his life—this is friendship. Friendship that needs to be achieved anew each day, so that it becomes ever deeper.

As a second answer, the Lord says this about the nature of friendship: "The servant does not know what his master is doing; but . . . all that I have heard from my Father I have made known to you" (Jn 15:15). Jesus' hearing the Father is not some sort of external process. It is the Son's whole existence. When he "makes known" what he "hears", we must reflect: like his "hearing", so too his "making known" is not merely speech, but, rather, his "making known" consists of the fact that he delivered himself to us to the point where he stands naked before us on the Cross, bares his whole being for us, and has no more secrets from us. In him, the Crucified One, we really see clear into the heart of God, the God who becomes weak for us, so that we can learn to live; the God whose inmost being is precisely his willingness to let himself be wounded for us. On the Cross, he is open and has no secrets left. Unless precisely this openness is his deepest secret. He told us everything; he opened himself up entirely to us. Our friendship in turn consists of the fact that we think and grow into this divine nature that is opened and delivered up to us in this way, so that it becomes increasingly the center of our knowledge and will and becomes our life, day by day.

All this is rounded out when we add to it two more key words from today's Gospel: the word "abide" (Jn 15:9-10, 16) and the word "joy" (Jn 15:11). These two terms are the characteristic leitmotifs that set the tone for this Gospel.

To abide means that a great start is not enough, the enthusiasm of a moment or of an early-morning hour, but rather the true friendship that is love matures in the patience of abiding. Often it may seem laborious, this abiding, too difficult for us, too opposed to our own will. But we know that ultimately we abide with ourselves only when we abide with him—in friendship. Therefore, we abide even when we fail. We abide because we know that he likes us, has accepted us: that precisely when we are weak, he especially loves us. We do not need to run away, then, but rather that is precisely when we must really take shelter in his friendship. He does not go away. He abides. Let us hold fast to him, just as he holds us. Then something worth lasting comes about: a life that can abide.

The other key word of today's Gospel is "joy". Joy is not comfort, just as blessedness is not the same as contentedness. Joy is more demanding. Joy ultimately consists of knowing how to go beyond the confines of our ego, being able to break down the barriers that hem us in; becoming one with him who holds the world together, with the Meaning [*Logos*] itself from which the world comes—with the Love that founds and sustains it. This emergence from the shackles of the ego and its pettiness, this being-freed into the greatness of all reality—this is joy, and it becomes all the greater, the more we learn to abide in friendship with Christ. In this we sense God's Yes to us. Our life stands in his Yes.

With that we have arrived at the concluding statement of today's reading. Paul says to the Corinthians: "We are not lords over your faith, but rather servants of your joy" (2 Cor 1:24, literal translation of the German version). If we are friends of Christ and remain in a communion of will with him, then we do not want to be lords over others. He himself, who really is the Lord of the world, willed to come to us, not under the banner of power, but rather as our servant. He still serves us, day by day, in the holy sacraments and through the grace of his word. Being his friend means becoming a servant with him. Only slavish souls find it necessary to lord it over others and to make excuses for their own lowliness with despotic gestures. Someone who has entered into the Lord's friendship does not need to play at being the lord. He will joyfully serve with him and acknowledge: There is nothing greater than to reveal to others, to hand on to others, the joy that has become ours: to lead people into God's great Yes.

Dear candidates for ordination, may it be granted to you to receive life and joy from this Yes and to be able to hand it on day by day. Your priestly life should be filled with it. From our hearts we all pray for that blessing for you in this hour.

To Stay United with Jesus—
Church as Communion
around the Altar

Ps 34:1–2, 15–22; Jn 6:60–69

Every Sunday liturgy of the Church is a little work of art, in which the words of the Old and the New Testament, prayers of Israel and prayers of the Church, are fitted together into a whole, which gives us not only new insights into God's revelation, but at the same time new prospects on our life, too, so that we have a better overview of it, see and understand it better, and in all the commotion of the many ways can find *the* Way, the path of life. Thus, today's liturgy with its readings and prayers, in which we find ourselves now, can help us to understand better the special, great, and glad event that has brought us together: the reopening of this church, the consecration of the new altar, and from it receive light for our everyday routine, also.

The key to the whole thing seems to me to be the prayer at the end of Mass, with which the Church will then lead us out in this same everyday routine. This prayer includes three petitions. The first one says: "Stay with us, O God, along the way with your redeeming mercy and perfect it." The second: "Make us courageous and generous in your love." And the third: "Let our will be conformed to yours."

I would like now to try simply to say something about each of these three petitions and to show how they are connected with what we are doing here now.

The first petition, then, says: "Perfect, O Lord, the word of your redeeming mercy." We all learned this in school and know it: We are redeemed. On the Cross, Jesus Christ unlocked for us once and for all the gate of salvation and granted redemption that is sufficient for the whole world and for all time. We are redeemed; redemption exists, but it has to arrive. And therefore it is not simply the past, but, rather, God's redeeming mercy is on the way throughout all of history in order to gather in everything in the world that is unredeemed: the afflictions, the sorrows, and the questions. God's mercy will be at an end only when the final hour of history arrives and the last tear is wiped away (Rev 7:17). Only then is it definitively true: We are redeemed.

And the altar that we have set up here is like a request to the Lord, like a hand outstretched toward him that says to him: Please do not forget this place of ours, either: Schönbrunn. Along the way of your mercies, come here, too, day by day. Gather in here, too, all the sorrow and all the need for love and kindness. Look at all the hearts that need you, at each quiet, unspoken call of what is unredeemed, at each prayer for mercy and kindness. Bring to a conclusion here, too, every day and every hour, the work of your redeeming mercy. Let us all be redeemed again and again starting from this place.

You built the altar, dear family of Schönbrunn. But in the consecration of the altar, we hand it over to God, and he gives it back to us again, so that now it is no longer only our prayer: "Do not overlook us on the way of your mercies." Instead, the altar is now an answer, too: "I am here, too, in this house, every day and every hour, perpetually. I see you all; I go to you all and am with each one."

From the most beautiful, magnificent altars of the cathedrals to the last, simplest altars somewhere in the primeval forest or to the hidden, temporary altars in places of persecution—all the altars of this world are such an answer from God, in which his redeeming mercy remains on the way perpetually, in which he perpetually says: "Here I am", in which he perpetually fulfills his promise: "From the cross I will draw all men to myself" (cf. Jn 12:32). Here he is, here his Cross is present, and his hands are outstretched to draw us all into his goodness, into his redeeming mercy. And the suffering that the Lord endured on the Cross is of course not just any human suffering. It is great and redemptive for us all because it is the suffering of the Son of God, because he drew all the suffering of the world into himself and into his transforming love. And we can all be certain: we stand in his sight; we have a place; he saw us, too, and blended our suffering into it. He accepts me, too, so as to perform the work of his redeeming mercy in me, too. So let us stop, as it were, again and again at this altar and ask him: "May it penetrate into me and may I be taken into your hands, so that your redeeming mercy may be perfected in me."

The second petition says: "Make us courageous and generous in your love." It actually describes everything that matters in the Christian life. The first thing is this: that before all our deeds and after all our deeds, we are loved by God and stand in his love. The first thing is not something that we must do; rather, the first thing is something that is given to me as a gift, something in which we are sheltered.

The Lord loves us, every one; no one is superfluous. There is no life that is not worth living, and there is no unimportant life. There is no accidental life that would be better off not existing. No, everyone can know: he willed me, too, and he loves me just as I am, and I am important in his plan for the world and for history, and this love does not abandon me unless *I* throw it away. In it I am sheltered. This is why Christian life is always first and foremost accepting the fact that we are loved.

And prayer, too, actually consists not so much of us telling God all sorts of things or giving him something that he did not yet have. Prayer consists of us allowing the fact that we are loved by God penetrate very deeply in us. This is actually how we should understand the celebration of the Eucharist, Holy Mass. It is not that *we* must do something. *He* is there and stretches out his hands, and we should experience Eucharist in such a way that we take this into ourselves deeply and allow ourselves to be permeated with this presence of his love.

The same is true for all other prayers. You have here now such a wonderful Way of the Cross, in which we can see all of this: the way that Jesus walked, following after all our afflictions and errors, picking us up again and again every time we fall. Praying the Way of the Cross or the Rosary means letting ourselves sink into this love, letting it fill us, recognizing, experiencing, and accepting it and thus being released and becoming free again.

And only from this receiving comes then our action,

and the prayer that I am talking about summarizes it in two fundamental qualities, namely, "brave" and "generous".

Brave does not mean that we have to scuffle. The bruiser is not the really brave man; rather, bravery consists above all in standing firm, being steadfast in our faith in love. There is so much in our life that might dissuade us from loving God. So much happens that we say: Why does he do this to me? Can he really still exist? It may happen that finally we remember only the negative things in the world and in life and that we thus allow ourselves to be torn away from the love of God.

Bravery consists of not letting ourselves be overcome by all these blows that we receive. That we remain with him. That we do not let the memory of what is good be stifled in us. That in all the adversity and evil and sorrow that we experience, we still keep the great treasure of the memories of what is good and beautiful in God's world and in our life, remain brave, and hold fast to him, do not let ourselves be driven away and thus remain faithful and consequently glad.

The world, after all, as we just heard in the Gospel, would like to dissuade us from the faith again and again and tell us: "All that just does not exist", and the Lord says: "Will you also go away?"

The bravery that he expects from us, based on the experience of his love, is that we say, like Peter: Lord, to whom should I go, then? You alone "have the words of eternal life" (Jn 6:68). You alone are the Holy One of God, the goodness of God; I am not going away, I am staying with you, because I know that that way I will stay in love!

From this bravery that remains with him, that does not let itself be driven away, then comes generosity. That is the other quality that God expects of us, just as he is generous. Many people today, when they do something for others, when they serve, are afraid that they are missing something in life, that then a piece of their own life is left unlived, for which they then have to compensate sometime. But the opposite is true. That same passion for life whereby we want to have it only for ourselves, makes us sadder and sadder, more and more empty. And every hour that we give away and devote to others is truly gained and makes us rich. The generosity with which we share our life and place it at the service of each other and of God is the only thing that gives us life. Only when we give it away, as the Lord says, is it returned to us a thousandfold; only then does life become life in the first place; only then can it succeed as life.

Here, too, the altar speaks to us again. I find it so wonderful, this generosity of God, that in every church, however small it may be, however poor it may be, and in the presence of every congregation, however distracted or forgetful it may be, he gives himself again and again and gives himself totally. He is so generous that he never considers it beneath him, not even in the most remote corner, and says, "Just a little is enough here. . . ." He gives himself! In this regard, God's generosity should penetrate our hearts again and again with its warmth and greatness and also give us this courage to be generous, based on his generosity, with the certainty that in this way we will find life.

And finally the last petition: "Conform our will to

yours." That is the description of what friendship is. Together to want the same thing and not to like the same
thing—that is what friends do. And so for us it would de-
pend on becoming friends of Jesus Christ, to come with
him in this fellowship of having the same taste, to like the
same things, and to reject the same things because they
are contrary to truth and contrary to love. We should try
to learn this communion of will with the Lord, so that
the commandments come no longer from outside, but
rather from this interior communion of will that unites
us with our Friend, with Jesus Christ.

The Divine Office that I chanted earlier expresses this
with somewhat different words. It says: "Grant that our
hearts may cast anchor at the place where there are true
joys." We are all seeking joy. A human being is born for
joy; we wish for joy. And many turn their backs on the
Church because they think that she is an obstacle to joy
and that only outside the Church or in opposition to her
can one find joy. But everyone nevertheless wishes this:
to stand, to be anchored so firmly in joy that nothing can
tear us from it anymore or make us sad and unhappy. But
ultimately joy can come only from being loved, and ultimately only in Jesus can this happen in a way that is altogether firm and sheltering for all human love. And so we
are then fastened to joy, so to speak, when we hold fast
to Jesus Christ. Then whatever may happen, somewhere
this light of joy from the inmost depths will be there, and
its luminous trail will also shed light on various sorts of
darkness.

This Sunday's liturgy illuminates this also with verses from a psalm, a promise to Israel, the full greatness

of which became comprehensible only in the light of
Jesus Christ. It says: "The LORD is near to the broken-
hearted. . . . Many are the afflictions of the righteous; but
the LORD delivers him out of them all. . . . Not one of
[his bones] is broken" (Ps 34:18–20). Saint John placed
this verse triumphantly at the end of his account of the
crucifixion (cf. Jn 19:36). Now here is someone whose
heart really is broken—they have pierced and opened it,
and his sorrow on our account has broken it from within.
Here is the one upon whom all the misfortune of the
world was laid and who is now dead and seems to be
utterly abandoned by God. And this is precisely when it
becomes evident that in all this it is nevertheless true of
him: God allows not one of his bones to be broken; he
rescues him entirely.

And this is true of us all, and from this we should experience again and again the fact that those who suffer,
those who lack something in their lives and who are bur-
dened by much misfortune, can be assured that they are
in his hands. He is close to their situation, and finally it
will be evident how he rescued us entirely in just that
way and that we can go, intact, into his hands and belong
to him completely.

And again the altar should tell us this: that *here* we have
the reliable point at which to anchor our joy, which no
one can take from us. And so, dear brothers and sisters,
you should see this altar that has been set up now as the
fixed point and anchoring point of joy. He is there, and
no one can take me from him, and he holds me in his
hands. To cast anchor here means: to be anchored at the

place where reliability and true joy are in the midst of the world's back and forth.

So let us thank the Lord on this day, that he gives us this sign of the answer, that with his mercy he remains on the way and is also perpetually present here. Let us thank him for sheltering us in his love and for constantly stretching out his hands, so as to draw us to himself and to shelter us in the place where the true joys are. And let us ask him that many blessings may proceed from this altar, from this church that is the center of your family, for many, many years to come.

Sources

Previously published homilies are listed with the corresponding number from the bibliography of Joseph Ratzinger's works: Joseph Ratzinger/Pope Benedict XVI, *Das Werk: Veröffentlichungen bis zur Papstwahl*, published by the *Schülerkreis* and edited by Vinzenz Pfnür (Augsburg: Paulinus Verlag, 2009) [hereafter abbreviated: Pfnür].

Homilies from the time of the pontificate were taken from the English translation at the Vatican website: http://w2.vatican.va/content/benedict-xvi/en.html.

What Holds It All Together—
Church as Foundation of Faith

Homily of Joseph Cardinal Ratzinger at the consecration of the parish church of Saint Albertus Magnus in Otto-brunn near Munich on October 2, 1977. Transcription of a tape recording, accessible online at www.albertusmagnus -archiv.de/pr_021077.htm.

The lecture by Wilhelm Stählin mentioned in the text was given on January 20, 1964, at a conference of the Martin-Luther-Gesellschaft in Münster and was published in: *Zur Auferbauung des Leibes Christi: Festgabe für Prof. Dr. Peter Brunner zum 65. Geburtstag*, edited by Edmund Schlink and Albrecht Peters (Kassel: Johannes Stauda-Verlag, 1965), 76–83. The citation from Saint Thérèse of Lisieux is taken from: *The Poetry of Saint Thérèse of Lisieux*, translated by Donald Kinney, O.C.D. (Washington, D.C.: ICS Publications, 1996), 119.

BAPTISM

The Light of Life

Homily by Joseph Cardinal Ratzinger at the Easter Vigil, April 14, 1979, in the Liebfrauendom in Munich. Transcription of a tape recording (Pfnür B_501).

Our Yes to Christ

Homily of Pope Benedict XVI during the celebration of Baptisms on the Feast of the Baptism of the Lord, January 8, 2006, in the Sistine Chapel in Rome.

CONFIRMATION

"Choose Life!"

Expanded version of a Confirmation homily by Joseph Cardinal Ratzinger, published as " 'Wähle das Leben': Eine Firmhomilie", in *Internationale Katholische Zeitschrift Communio* 11 (1982): 444–49 (Pfnür B_683).

Sealed with the Spirit

Homily of Pope Benedict XVI at the Eucharistic Celebration on the Occasion of the 23rd World Youth Day, Sunday, July 20, 2008, at the Randwick Racecourse, Australia.

CONFESSION

Be Reconciled with God

Homily by Joseph Cardinal Ratzinger at a Mass for Bavarian pilgrims in the Extraordinary Holy Year on May 24, 1983, in Saint Peter's Basilica in Rome. Published as "Versöhnung, auf die wir alle warten" in the German edition of *L'Osservatore Romano* 13, no. 24 (1983): 14. The text was revised and slightly abridged for publication.

He Restores to Us Our Dignity as His Children

Homily of Pope Benedict XVI on the occasion of his visit to the prison for minors, "Casa del Marmo", in Rome on March 18, 2007.

HOLY EUCHARIST

Transformation Occurs in Prayer

Homily of Pope Benedict XVI on Holy Thursday during the Mass of the Lord's Supper, April 9, 2009, in the Basilica of Saint John Lateran in Rome.

In Bread and Wine He Gives Himself Entirely

Homily of Pope Benedict XVI during Holy Mass on Saint John Lateran Square on the Solemnity of the Sacred Body and Blood of Christ, June 15, 2006.

ANOINTING OF THE SICK

Living by God's Great Love

Homily of Joseph Cardinal Ratzinger at a liturgy for disabled people on October 31, 1981, in the Theatine Church of Saint Cajetan in Munich. Published in the *Münchener Ordinariats-Korrespondenz* 35 (November 5, 1981). The text was slightly abridged for publication (Pfnür B_639).

Abandoning Oneself to God's Mercy

Homily of Pope Benedict XVI during the Eucharistic Celebration in Lourdes on September 15, 2008, the Memorial of Our Lady of Sorrows, during his Apostolic Journey to France.

MATRIMONY

Maturing in Love

Homily by Joseph Cardinal Ratzinger at the Wedding of Anne Richardi and Stefan Strehler on August 31, 1991, in the Church of the Assumption of Mary in Regensburg. Transcript of a tape recording. Made available by Prof. Dr. Reinhard Richardi, Pentling.

To Love Means to Give Oneself

Homily by Joseph Cardinal Ratzinger at the Wedding of Anthony and Marta Valle on June 24, 2004, the Solemnity of the Birth of Saint John the Baptist, in Saint Peter's Basilica in Rome. The homily was originally given in German, recorded, translated very informally into English and made available by Anthony Valle. It was translated back into German by Dr. Manuel Schlögl. That German text is the basis for the English translation in this volume.

HOLY ORDERS

Follow—Leave—Proclaim

Homily by Joseph Cardinal Ratzinger at the Priestly Ordination of the Graduates of the Collegium Germanicum et Hungaricum on October 10, 1989, in San Ignazio in Rome. Published in: *Korrespondenzblatt des Collegium Germanicum et Hungaricum* 96 (1990): 40–44.

I No Longer Call You Servants, but Friends

Homily by Joseph Cardinal Ratzinger at the Priestly Ordination of the Graduates of the Collegium Germanicum et Hungaricum on October 10, 1996, in San Ignazio in Rome. Published in: *Korrespondenzblatt des Collegium Germanicum et Hungaricum* 103 (1997): 43–47.

I am grateful to Prof. Dr. Armin Wildfeuer of St. Augustin for providing the two ordination homilies.

To Stay United with Jesus—Church as Communion around the Altar

Homily by Joseph Cardinal Ratzinger at the reopening of Saint Joseph Church in Schönbrunn (Archdiocese of Munich and Freising) and the consecration of its altar on August 25, 1985. Transcription of an audio recording (Pfnür B_749).